Bitcoin For Mere Mortals

...and for those who want to change the world

Disclaimer:

Nothing in this book is financial advice, do your own research and make your own decisions. Never invest what you can't afford to lose, and always invest for the long run.

Written in October 2021

Introduction

I'm going to take a wild shot here and presume that you are broke or at least not as wealthy as you would like to be. This is how I define poor: If you have to go to work every day to a job you dislike, to earn just enough to pay the bills while daydreaming about retirement, spare time, and freedom, then you haven't made it yet.

It's not your fault. All your life you've done the right thing. You went to school, got good grades, got a decent job, and worked hard. Yet, you are 2 months away from destitution. If you lose your job today, how long could you survive? How long before you lose your house, your car, your family, and your dignity?

Not long I guess. You've done your bit but the system keeps moving the goalposts farther and farther away and no matter how fast you run, you are always behind.

You are not alone. The middle class has been losing purchasing power since the 70s. Prices keep escalating but salaries remain stagnant. A career for life or even a decent job, are things of the past. Globalization, automation, and relocation are constant threats to our standards of living.

Not only do you have to work for 60 hours a week just to make ends meet, but when you get home, you have to retrain yourself to be ready for the day they sack you with no compensation and become unemployable.

And then, there is the pension thing. Oh dear, don't get me started. If you think you're going to see a dime of all the thousands you poured into your pension scheme, you're delusional. When you get to that age, there will be nothing left. They call it a scheme for a reason.

But it's not all bad news. There is some hope.

The current monetary system of Fiat money, easy debt, and infinite supply is broken. In fact, it never actually worked. We've been borrowing money from the future and now it's payback time.

Luckily there is an alternative. There is a new currency that is not printed by the government, that central banks can't control, and that has a very limited supply that can't be manipulated.

It is like money, only better. It doesn't suffer from inflation, devaluation, corruption, or censorship. It is decentralized, transparent, immutable, and permissionless.

It is a new way to redistribute wealth that benefits everyone equally. It's an open system that promises fairness, transparency, and strict rules that can't be bent by the powerful.

It can bring social justice, a greener planet, less violence, and more equality. It is the best opportunity for the third world to escape poverty and for the middle class to live a more abundant and fulfilling life.

It means freedom, peace, and justice.

This system is of course Bitcoin.

You might have heard about bitcoin in the media, from politicians, bankers, or from internet trolls but let me tell you, most of those do not have a clue about what this is all about, and even those who do, are too scared of losing their privileges to have an objective view.

But what's in it for you? You might be asking.

Are you tired of working hours on end with nothing to show for it?

Are you buried in a mountain of debt that will never be able to repay?

Aren't you sick of living like a hermit only for the bank and the taxman to take most of your earnings?

Would you like to escape the rat race once and for all?

Would you like to take a year off and travel to exotic locations?

Do you think there is a chance your dreams might come true one day?

Then carry on reading.

Who am I?

I'm a Bitcoin aficionado that entered the space in 2013. Ever since, I've been studying the market, the possibilities, and the potential of this new monetary system.

At first, I was attracted to the quick gains but then I discovered there was much more to it. It's a proper way to handle finances, away from crony politicians, corrupt bankers, and legacy systems.

I became so fascinated with it, that I have devoted many hours a day to studying it deeply. After 1000 hours, I feel I haven't even begun to scratch the surface so I keep going down the rabbit hole daily.

But don't be put off by this. You don't need to become an expert to be able to benefit from this system. In the same way that you don't know how the internet works, and yet, you are able to use it proficiently, you can become a user and benefit from bitcoin without knowing all the technicalities.

In this book, I try to explain in plain English what bitcoin and other crypto are, why it is a sound system and how you can benefit immensely from it.

If at the end of the book you have a better grasp of this ecosystem and are able to make informed decisions, financial or otherwise, my mission will be fulfilled.

Who are you?

You are a person who is smart enough to realize that this system of banks, Fiat money, debt, and pensions is broken. You've been looking for an alternative to secure your financial future but so far you have found none.

You've heard about this new digital currency but don't quite know what to make of it. The scaremongers are telling you to stay away from it, but you think they might have vested interests.

You are curious about an alternative to the current system and want to know more about it. Keep reading and you'll understand it better.

Why did I write this book?

Every time I tell my friends about bitcoin, I see many misunderstandings, confusion, and misperceptions.

Most of these have been triggered by fear. The media has mastered the art of scaremongering in order to get your attention. People in power don't welcome change, they have too much to lose, so any opportunity and platform available, it's used to create confusion, fear, and doubt (FUD) in order to delay the inevitable.

I've always had a penchant for technology, science, and progress. Every time I discover a new trend, I study its potential and try to project it into the future. Most people are not like this, I find. They rather bury their heads in the sand and prefer to think that we've already progressed enough and things will remain more or less the same. This is known as the end of history illusion.

Here's an example from the past I find fascinating:

Easter morning 1900: 5th Ave, New York City. Spot the automobile.

Source: US National Archives.

In 1900, there were almost no automobiles on 5th Ave. Fast forward 13 years:

**Easter morning 1913: 5th Ave, New York City.
Spot the horse.**

Source: George Grantham Bain Collection.

No horses.

This shows how fast technology can take over the world and change our lives.

Yet, this huge change happened despite the Luddites. Lots of so-called experts said the automobile was too noisy, too slow, too expensive, and too polluting to succeed. One entrepreneur went as far as betting all of his fortune to acquire 5000 horses to demonstrate his commitment to the good old technology.

Needless to say, he went bankrupt. Blindness to anticipate the future is a death sentence. That's why it's important to spot trends, anticipate the outcomes, and get well-positioned to take advantage of the wave.

Bitcoin is a tsunami that is taking all over the world. You either get out of the way, learn to surf it, or will be swallowed by it.

Whether you agree with it or not, it will affect your life, your work, and your finances. In the same way, the internet, smartphones, or AI have transformed every industry, Bitcoin will shift your reality and disrupt your life in unpredictable ways.

Bitcoin is a disruptive technology that aims to transform banking, trading, and the way we deal with money. All these legacy systems could well end up like the horse and buggies of 5th avenue; relegated to a museum for the amazement of future generations.

The internet has disrupted many industries but so far has spared financial institutions. Now, they are starting to worry about the bitcoin tsunami coming their way.

In 2030, the world will be a very different place and most of the changes will come from the bitcoinazation of society.

You can learn about this technology now and benefit from it, or join the horse guy in New York.

Your choice.

Terminology

The crypto world, like any other specialized field, comes with its own lingo but don't be put off by it. It's just a few words you will hear again and again until they become familiar.

Feel free to skip this section if it becomes too overwhelming. Just by reading the book, these concepts will become self-evident.

In this book, I have decided to use the dollar and the American terminology for simplicity. If you deal with other currencies you will have to translate these numbers to your local system.

Bitcoin

Decentralized digital currency supported by a distributed network of nodes that allows payments to be sent directly on a peer-to-peer basis and without the need for a trusted third party.

Ethereum

The second cryptocurrency by market cap was co-created by Vitalik Buterin based on a programmable platform that allows the implementation of Smart Contracts, Dapps, DAOs, and NFTs.

Fiat money

Money that is not backed by anything apart from the trust in the system of central banks and governments. Most of the currencies we know and use daily belong to this category - the US dollar, the British Pound, The Euro, the Yen, etc.

The current version of Fiat money was introduced by Richard Nixon in 1971 when he decided to break the link between the dollar and gold.

Fiat money can be printed limitlessly since it is not backed by anything and this creates serious problems for the economy like inflation, devaluation, and debasement.

Blockchain

A decentralized, distributed public ledger where transactions get recorded in blocks that store data in an immutable, transparent, and secure way.

This public ledger records transactions that get verified by the network and then get stamped chronologically. This data gets distributed in thousands of nodes around the world, each maintaining identical copies of the records, making the system extremely secure and hackerproof.

The blockchain can record any type of data, not just financial. Identity proof, notary services, traceability, electronic voting system, and many more are some of the application for this new technology.

Stablecoins

Cryptocurrencies have a stable value that it's usually pegged to the dollar. USDC, Tether, and Dai are some examples and their value stays close to $1 permanently.

Sablecoins get rid of the volatility and provide a platform for lending, borrowing, and trading that serves as a bridge between the fiat and the crypto worlds.

DeFi

Decentralized Finance. Defi is an umbrella term for all financial transactions that can be done in a decentralized way without the intervention of a trusted third party.

For example, two peers could borrow and lend money to each other by using a decentralized exchange like compound without the need for intermediaries.

Smart Contract

A smart contract is an agreement between two parties that get coded in the blockchain and that forces both parties to fulfill their contractual obligations.

An analogy often used to explain this concept is vending machines. You put the money in, you get the Coke. There is no leeway, no interpretation, and no bargaining. The contract is written in stone and gets fulfilled automatically.

Smart contracts have many applications like insurance, mortgages, property ownership and trading, and can revolutionize many industries speeding up processes and reducing legal burdens.

FUD

Fear, Uncertainty, and Doubt. Propaganda used by the media, politicians, and bankers to scare the public and delay cryptocurrency adoption.

Bitcoin takes power away from the state and the fat cats react by spreading lies. Don't believe a word they say.

FOMO

Fear Of Missing Out. When people see Bitcoin going up they can't help but chase the trend and rush to buy some coins.

However, this is not a good idea. Investment decisions should be cold and calculated. There is no rush.

DCA

Dollar-Cost Averaging is one of the best strategies for investing. It consists of buying small amounts regularly regardless of the price. This way emotions are removed from the process and decisions become more rational.

Peer to Peer

From person to person directly without the intervention of a third party. Like Bittorrent or Emule.

Nodes

Computers that runs the bitcoin code and stores a copy of the blockchain. The bitcoin network is run by thousands of nodes and the number keeps growing. This creates a network effect that makes bitcoin very resilient.

Miners

Specific types of nodes that verify every operation and also compete with each other to create (mine) new coins. Right now, 900 bitcoins are mined daily and this will be reduced by half in 2024.

Hash

A hash function is a cryptographic code that runs uni-directionally validating the authenticity and integrity of the input. SHA256 is the specific function used in the bitcoin network.

Wallet

An App or physical device that allows users to store the private keys to access their digital access in the blockchain. There are hot and cold wallets. Cold wallets are offline and therefore more secure.

HODL

Buy bitcoin and never sell it.

Exchanges

Online platforms where cryptocurrencies can be bought and sold using Fiat or any other currency. Some of the best are Kraken, Binance and Coinbase.

Satoshis

Fraction of bitcoin that divides it by 100 million. Thus 1 BTC = 100,000,000 Satoshis

FAQs

Being such a nascent technology and revolutionary concept, it is normal to have many questions and doubts about it. Here are some of the most common ones.

Who backs Bitcoin?

Bitcoin is backed by math, cryptography, the algorithm, and the blockchain.

The decentralized network serves as a base layer to run the system and the nodes and miners verify the integrity of the transactions.

There is no centralized operation, headquarters, or leader. All is done in a distributed manner making the system very robust.

Is it a scam?

A decentralized network can't ever be a scam because no one is in charge and nobody benefits directly from the bitcoin success. Besides, the rules of the network are immutable, transparent, and tamper-free.

Fiat money, on the other hand, could be considered a scam because it is printing money out of thin air, benefiting a small elite and bending the rules to their advantage.

Who created Bitcoin?

Satoshi Nakamoto is the pseudonymous name of bitcoin's inventor. Nobody knows who he/she/they really are. They probably decided to keep anonymity in order to protect themselves from powerful enemies that wouldn't like this new asset class.

How to get it?

Usually, bitcoin and other cryptos are traded in exchanges like Kraken, Binance or Coinbase. It's just a matter of sending some dollars and then buying the coins of your choice in a similar fashion as it's done with online brokers.

How to make profits?

Buying low and selling high, like in the stock market. However, with crypto, it's advisable to hold it for much longer to enjoy the appreciation.

What about tax?

Selling Bitcoin for a profit incurs capital gains that are taxable. You should declare it as such and pay tax accordingly. Bitcoin is treated as property meaning only realized capital gains are taxable.

When should I sell them?

Never. Bitcoin is the most pristine asset ever and will keep appreciating forever. The moment you sell, it'll go 20x and you'll regret it.

So, what's the point of investing if I don't sell?
Like with any asset, you can still enjoy its appreciation without selling it. Wealthy individuals that own real estate, stocks, or gold never sell it, when they need cash, they just borrow against it and use it as collateral.

I can't afford Bitcoin. Should I buy a cheaper coin?

No. Bitcoin is at this price for a reason. It's the best cryptocurrency, it's the best store of value, and due to the network effect and scarcity, it will continue appreciating forever.

Most of the Altcoins are garbage and will disappear soon. Besides, you don't need to buy a full Bitcoin. It's better to own 0.001 BTC than 1000 Dogecoin. Bitcoin is the safest bet and the one with the most potential. Don't be deluded by shiny objects.

Should I wait until it drops to enter?

Well, bitcoin is volatile, and every now and then it experiences some drops but you have to be very quick to take advantage of those or use automated trading to buy the dips.

Some people sold when it was at $20,000 and are still waiting to reenter the market. They could be waiting forever.

Chances are BTC's price will reach $100,000 soon and then we might never see it below $60,000.

Is it a good idea to trade (buy the dips, sell the tops) in order to increase profits?

No. Trading is extremely hard and very few people can manage it successfully. Besides, it takes a toll on your body and mind. It's just easier to buy and HODL.

What's the best strategy to invest in?

Dollar-Cost Averaging combined with buying the dips.

With DCA, you buy a small amount every month regardless of the price, and then, when it drops, you buy more. Nothing can beat this strategy in the long run.

Should I invest in Dogecoin, Shiba Inu, and any of the other silly coins?

No, unless you want to throw your money away. Buy quality and not garbage.

How can I trust something that it's not tangible like gold or money?

Most assets nowadays are not tangible. Gold is bought in paper form and you never get to see it. 90% of the dollars in circulation exist only in digital form. Apple, Google, Amazon are some of the most valuable companies in the world and are mostly virtual.

We live in the digital world and it makes sense to hold digital assets. Welcome to the 21st century.

Is it a bubble?

Bubbles don't usually last for 12 years, are not bought by Publicly traded companies or governments, and are not global phenomenon.

Bitcoin is not a bubble because it is scarce, decentralized, and provides an excellent store of value. The market appreciates this and thus the demand keeps growing. The internet wasn't a bubble either although many self-proclaimed experts accused it of being so.

Can it be banned?

Bitcoin is the most decentralized network ever created so it can't effectively be banned unless the whole internet goes off forever. And if this ever happens, we'll have bigger problems to worry about.

They have tried to ban it in China and other places but anyone with access to the internet and using a VPN can buy and sell bitcoin without much problem. Besides, it's now too big to be banned. Banks, public traded companies, and wealthy individuals own it and these have a say in the regulations.

Isn't it too expensive already?

Bitcoin was already too expensive at $1
Then, it was too expensive at $10
Then, the same at $100
Then, at $1000
Then at $10,000
Now, it's expensive at $55,000
Then, It'll be expensive at $100,000
And so on…

Bitcoin is always expensive when looking back but cheap when looking forward.

Due to the increasing demand and the scarcity, the potential for growth is huge. We are still very early, only about 1.5% of the world owns bitcoin. This is like the internet in the 90s. So no, it's not expensive at all. It's a screaming bargain.

But I can't afford a whole bitcoin!

You don't need to buy a full bitcoin, you can start from $10 which is 0.00018 BTC or 18,000 Satoshis.

How can I protect my Bitcoin?

The safest approach is to buy a cold wallet like Trezor or Ledger and then store it in a safe place. Doing it this way, your money will be safer than in the bank.

But isn't all this too risky?

No. What is very risky is trusting your future to Fiat money, banks, and obsolete financial institutions. By doing so you are putting all your eggs in one basket and that basket is broken.

Holding cash is dangerous right now, high inflation is coming. You should diversify into other assets and bitcoin is just one of them.

Where can I find reliable information about crypto?

There are a number of channels and books that I follow and recommend:

- The Bitcoin whitepaper
- What Bitcoin did
- Michael Saylor (www.hope.com)
- Invest answers (Youtube)
- Saifedean Ammous (The Bitcoin Standard)
- Andreas Antonopoulos (Mastering Bitcoin)
- Crypto R us (YouTube)

Chapter 1

What is Bitcoin?

Bitcoin is a form of electronic cash that allows the transfer of value between parties without the intervention of a trusted third party like a bank.

This decentralized nature and peer-to-peer basis might seem trivial at first, but it's actually one of the main features of bitcoin vs Fiat money.

In order to make this permissionless system work, while solving old age obstacles like the double-spending or the Byzantines general problem, Bitcoin uses elegant solutions like the blockchain, proof of work, and cryptography. Don't worry too much about this jargon, it'll be explained later.

Money, as we know it, is very centralized. In order for you to make a transaction, a bank or a credit card company has to act as an intermediary supervising the operation and making sure you have enough balance in your account. This is achieved by using a central database where all the customer's data gets stored with instant settlements to ensure the integrity of the transaction.

A centralized system is often more efficient than a centralized one, but it's also less secure. A central database offers counterparty risks and a single point of failure that can easily be attacked by hackers or ill-intentioned actors.

Bitcoin is supported by an ever-expanding decentralized network of nodes which ensures continuity even if part of the network goes down. Unlike centralized systems, there is no single point of failure and no honeypot to attack. This makes bitcoin extremely robust and antifragile.

Origins

Bitcoin was created in 2008 by Satoshi Nakamoto (who decided to remain anonymous) as a reaction to the bailouts given by the governments to banks after the subprime mortgage collapse.

Certainly, Nakamoto had a point. It seems very unfair that banks take on huge risks in order to make money only to be rescued by the taxpayer when things go wrong.

Nakamoto regarded centralized monetary systems, governments' unlimited debt, and obsolete banking institutions as dangerous, corrupt, and inefficient. There has to be a better way to do things in the 21st century.

Satoshi released the Bitcoin Whitepaper in a cryptography forum in 2008. Here, he explains how it is possible to create an alternative to the current financial system where trust, intermediaries, and permissions are not necessary. The whitepaper is the work of a genius, I encourage you to read it. It's only 9 pages and not that technical either.

These are some of the elements of this technology.

Miners

In order to create bitcoin, first, it has to be mined. Mining is done by specialized powerful computers that compete to solve mathematical puzzles where the winner gets to mine one block containing a number of bitcoins.

This way, the system creates a constraint (the computational power) as well as a financial incentive (the bitcoins mined).

Miners collect all those bitcoins as a reward and make a profit once they have discounted the amortization of the equipment and the electricity used.

Electricity is the second constraint, these powerful computers are known as ASICs, use a fair amount of electricity but this is so by design. Nakamoto knew that there had to be a cost involved, otherwise it would become too easy to create new coins and the system would implode by an excess of supply.

This electricity usage has been criticized by many but in reality, this energy is not wasted, it's stored in every coin. In this sense, it could be argued that bitcoin is a giant battery that stores energy as monetary value. More on that later.

Halving

Every 4 years, the number of bitcoin contained in a block gets cut by half. Right now, successful miners obtain 6.25 BTC per block. 1 block gets mined every 10 mins so every day a total of 900 BTCs are released into the market. This supply will be cut by half in 2024.

This halving ensures the flow of new coins gets reduced over time, making bitcoin even more scarce than it already is.

The number of bitcoins that will ever exist is capped at 21 million of which 18.8 million are already in circulation.

This scarcity and diminishing flow affect the BTC's market price making the system self-adjusting and ensuring that difficulty mining and rewards are always checked in balance.

The algorithm

Bitcoin uses the cryptographic hash algorithm SHA-256 in order to verify transactions and calculate the Proof of Work mechanism.

SHA-256 is regarded as one of the safest cryptographic functions to protect a system. This along with the zero-knowledge proof and the decentralized network makes bitcoin almost invulnerable.

In 12 years, no one has been able to hack the system or do an illegal transaction despite the amount of monetary value held in the blockchain. In comparison, most centralized systems like the CIA, the FBI, the FED, and Commercial banks have been hacked one way or another. This shows the invulnerability of decentralized systems.

Who is in charge?

No one. This is the beauty of it.

Satoshi Nakamoto moved on to other projects a couple of years after the release of bitcoin and now the algorithm, the rules in place, and the consensus mechanism, make the system work with very little human intervention.

Let's face it, humans don't know how to handle money and power. This is why we have all the financial turmoil every few years. When the system, the algorithm, and the rules are working, it is best not to interfere. We, humans, are inefficient and corrupt by nature. Bitcoin offers a predictable monetary policy and a very reliable way to store value.

The bitcoin network is supported by thousands of independent nodes that follow exactly the same rules and that are incentivized to keep the system working. Bitcoin is considered the most secure network ever created.

The Blockchain

In order to record transactions permanently, the nodes generate multiple copies of every operation in a public ledger known as the blockchain.

You could think of the blockchain as a public book of transactions that is transparent, immutable, and permanent. Thousands of identical copies of this book are kept to protect the integrity of the system and avoid tampering.

Every transaction gets recorded chronologically and time-stamped in a way that the longest chain with the most copies is the valid one in case of a dispute.

In a process known as confirmation, miners endorse the validity of the operation. After 6 confirmations, the transaction becomes immutable.

The blockchain is known as trustless technology because it doesn't need trust in a third party to ensure the validity of the process. Verification is a much more secure procedure and this is done by the algorithm automatically.

The blockchain has many uses apart from recording financial transactions. It is used among other things for ID verification, electronic voting, food traceability, notary records, etc. There is a whole new industry based on this public ledger recording technology.

Just to understand how secure the blockchain is, let's see an example. A few years ago, China was trying to destroy the film database of the Hongkong television network. To avoid this, some activists uploaded the metadata of these videos into the blockchain. As a result, these records will stay there forever, not even mighty China with all its censorship power can't alter those records. Nothing can beat the blockchain.

The double-spending problem

In order to make a monetary system work, the first problem we encounter is how to avoid the double-spending problem or the possibility that the same money gets spent twice.

With cash, this is easy to solve. Once you buy the goods, you part with the money and this creates instant settlement.

With Digital money, this is not so straightforward. Banks solve this problem through a centralized database, instant settlement, and fast communication between the terminals. Account balances get updated immediately, preventing anyone from spending the same money twice.

In a decentralized system like bitcoin, this is achieved through the blockchain. Once you spend your money, there is a public record confirmed by the nodes that stop any spent bitcoin from further use. This system is known as UTXO.

Trustless system

Bitcoin doesn't need to rely on trust, a third party, or any form of external supervision. Everything gets verified by the nodes and then written in stone in the blockchain.

Don't trust, verify is the motto often heard in the crypto community and it's one of the main selling points of Bitcoin.

What is backing bitcoin?

Bitcoin is backed by the blockchain, maths, cryptography, and the algorithm. All these are immutable systems that can't be manipulated, hacked, or censored.

In contrast, the US Dollar or the Euro are backed by the trust we put in central banks and governments. How much do you trust bankers and politicians? Not a lot? I wonder why.

In reality, Fiat money is backed by debt. Governments print money, increase the debt ceiling, and kick the can down the road. They behave like an irresponsible consumer maxing out one credit card and using another to pay the debt. The whole system is a house of cards that is ready to collapse.

How is bitcoin regulated?

Bitcoin works pretty much outside the system, it's very difficult to regulate, ban or restrict it.

In most jurisdictions, bitcoin is considered an asset and thus subject to capital gains.

This is one of the reasons HODLers buy and never sell, so they don't trigger a taxable event.

Governments all over the world have been trying to regulate bitcoin to a certain extent, but due to its decentralized nature, this is very difficult to achieve. For example, bitcoin adoption in China is quite high despite getting banned every year.

Bitcoin as a digital asset

We are moving quickly into a digital world. The old cash system is disappearing fast. Some people object that they prefer tangible assets like money or gold rather than purely digital ones. But this is actually a fallacy.

Most valuable assets are already online; Apple, Amazon, Google, or Facebook are mostly digital also, and yet, these companies own the world. 20 years ago everything was offline, now we spend more than half of our time online. We are moving from the analog to the digital world and this trend is only going to accelerate.

In this digital world, we need digital assets and these are as valuable as their physical counterparts. Ask any kid if they regard something they built in Fornite or Minecraft as valuable and you'll see. Intangible assets can be worth a lot.

Fiat money

The money you use on a daily basis is not as reliable, secure, or efficient as you might think. In order to understand bitcoin, first, you need to understand Fiat money so you can compare both systems and decide which is better.

But that's for the next chapter.

Chapter 2

Fiat Money

Often bitcoin gets rejected as too complex, too technical, and too obscure to be understood. While this is a valid critique, we often don't realize how complex the traditional monetary system is. One thing is to use the money on a daily basis, and another is understanding how the system really works.

Fiat money (Dollar, Euro, Yen, etc) is money created by decree. The current version of Fiat money started 50 years ago. Richard Nixon decided in 1971 to abandon the gold standard ending up the peg between the US dollar and the gold reserves held by the Federal Reserve.

This was the beginning of a new era. From then onwards, money became infinite. It can be printed limitlessly without any backing, restriction, or cap. Central banks all over the world can create money out of thin air and flood the markets with liquidity as they see fit.

Printing money this way leads to the debasement of the currency, inflation, and to an unpredictable monetary supply. No one knows how much money will be printed this year, how much real inflation we have, and how all this affects the bigger picture of the economy.

This year alone, $8 Trillion dollars have been printed by the FED increasing the money supply by 40%. Central banks have the power to create money out of thin air and they use it to boost the economy.

But there is a caveat. The higher the money supply, the less value it has, meaning that all the dollars in your bank account get devalued and you become poorer.

By working hard, you are trading your most valuable asset - time - for money. However, as more money gets printed, it's worthless so you've wasted your time. Inflation is theft. Effectively, when they destroy value, they are also destroying your time.

The US Dollar has lost 98% of its value since 1913 and this has been mostly due to the inflation provoked by overprinting. Every time there is a crisis, a war, or a need to stimulate the economy, the money printing machines start rolling and this creates an oversupply that leads to the debasement of the currency.

National debt, inflation, quantitative easing, pension schemes, interest rates, and money supply are just some concepts created by the current monetary system and that very few people, including economists, understand well.

So before you reject bitcoin as a complex subject, realize that the money you use daily is a far more complicated system that's designed to keep you poor, enslaved, and fearful.

Venezuela is an extreme case of how a wealthy country can go bankrupt by printing too much money. Let it serve as a warning of the dangers of a loose monetary policy.

Fiat money is not as solid as we are led to believe. On average, Fiat currencies' life expectancy is just about 27 years. The German

Mark, for example, was replaced by a new currency 3 times during the 20th century.

Every time there is a war, a big devaluation, or a crisis, governments decide to scrap the currency and start all over with new Fiat money and hope this time things will work out. But it never does.

The longest surviving currency is the British pound with a few centuries behind it, but it has lost most of its purchasing power since its inception. The reason it is called sterling is because one pound could buy an ounce of silver (about half a kilo). Now, it's not possible to buy almost anything with £1.

So be careful with your Fiat money. First, it can be debased overnight. Second, it could be taken out of circulation following a currency collapse, and third, inflation is eating away your wealth slowly but surely.

There are two leagues in the Fiat system. On one hand, we have the top currencies: the dollar, euro, Pound, Yen, and a few others. On the other hand, we have the rest.

If proper currencies suffer from inflation, debasement, and oversupply, the rest have much deeper problems.

Almost any currency in Africa, Latin America, and most parts of Asia are worthless. They suffer from hyperinflation, devaluation, confiscation, censorship, and corruption. The horror stories we hear in the news about Venezuela, Zimbabwe, Argentina, and many other countries are a sad reality that their citizens have to deal with on a daily basis.

Would you like to be paid in Sudanese Pounds, Zimbabwean dollars, or Vietnamese Dongs? Me neither. I rather not work than have to deal with money that can't hold any value.

I visited Caracas in 2002, I had a beer and paid a few Bolivars for it. Now that same beer costs 2 million Bolivars. That's inflation.

Inflation

In the 70s, my father bought a brand new car, a Seat 127 for 160,000 pesetas (1000€). 3 years and 100,000 km later, he sold it for exactly the same amount. By that time, the new model had doubled in price. That's inflation.

The 70s were a high inflationary decade even for strong currencies like the dollar. 15-20% was the average annually. We could well be heading towards a similar situation prompted by the never-ending money printing during the current crisis.

Printing money is an emergency measure to stimulate the economy. It certainly injects liquidity and encourages consumption in the short term, but in the long run, it devalues the currency and damages the economy.

Printing money is theft. You work hard in order to save money and then it gets debased by the government by pressing a button. All that time you spent at the office has now become worthless because somebody decided to make money more abundant.

When the money supply increases by 30%, your money is automatically worth 30%. All of a sudden bread, milk, petrol, wood, electricity become more expensive and generally, your salary just won't keep up.

Inflation is one of the biggest flaws of Fiat money but not the only one. Here are some others:

- Confiscation. Your country has the legal right to take all the money in your bank account for any reason they deemed necessary and there is nothing you can do about it
- Devaluation. Governments can and do devalue their currency overnight by decree. Argentina has suffered 20 devaluations in recent history, some of them 100:1
- Forced exchange. Even if you keep other currencies in your bank account, like dollars, the government can force you to exchange those for the local currency at any rate they dictate. Again Argentina

Most of these examples come from developing nations but even in the first world, your money is not as safe as you think.

In Europe and the US, inflation is generally kept under 5% and the cases of devaluation and confiscation are rare. However, let's not relax. We are facing one of the biggest crises in history and anything could happen. Even in the best-case scenario, a 5% inflation means your money becomes half in less than 10 years.

Human rights, international law, and tacit agreements are respected until they are not. Everything is more fragile than it seems. Don't trust, verify.

Banks

The current monetary system is linked to the banking industry and these are not to be trusted either. The inefficiencies, the fees, the bureaucracy, and the rejections are daily occurrences we are too familiar with.

For example, if you send money internationally, it will take up to 3 working days to clear. Even FedEx is faster than this. Maybe they didn't get the memo that an electronic transaction travels at the speed of light.

Unfortunately, we don't have a choice. If you want to keep your money safe, use credit cards, have access to credit and some investments, you have to endure the pain of such an inefficient system...

Unless…

As with Fiat money, banks in the first world are way better than banks in developing nations. In fact, in many countries, most people don't even have access to a bank. These are known as the unbanked.

But even in the industrialized world, there is a technology that is threatening to compete with the banking services provided by traditional financial institutions. An asset that could solve most of the inefficiencies and flaws of Fiat money and the banking industry. A currency that is not infinite, non-manipulable, non-confiscatable, or non-censorable. A system that is decentralized, transparent, and immutable.

Let's have a look.

Chapter 3

Bitcoin as an Investment

Bitcoin, unlike Fiat money, has a supply cap of 21 million, it's not controlled or manipulated by any government and the transactions are immutable, transparent, and irreversible.

What's the point of Bitcoin?

Bitcoin has utility as an investment, as a store of value, as protection against devaluation, inflation, and confiscation, and many other advantages that will keep developing as the technology advances.

Inflation

Bitcoin is anti-inflationary due to the limited supply. Since demand keeps growing, this produces a supply shock making its price go exponential.

In this sense, it's similar to gold, scarce, and with a high stock-to-flow ratio.

Fiat money is inflationary, especially during periods of heavy money printing, and therefore it makes a poor store of value.

During turbulent times, most investors look for safe havens to protect their wealth. Gold has traditionally been the vehicle of choice, but recently the yellow metal is losing its luster.

Bitcoin has been appreciating 200% a year for the last 12 years and although this rate will eventually slow down, most experts agree that it could reach $1 Million by 2030.

In 12 years of existence, BTC has gone from 0 to $60,000 reaching a total market cap of $1 Trillion.

No other asset has been able to achieve that feat in such a short time. It took Google, Apple, or Amazon much longer to get to the Trillion mark.

Among the Bitcoin investors, there are poor people in developing countries, wealthy individuals, and institutions in the industrialized world. The adoption is still very low - less than 1% - so we are still early and the potential is unlimited. It's been named **the best asymmetric bet of our lifetime.**

Here's a stock-to-flow model from PlanB that has been able to predict BTC's price accurately so far.

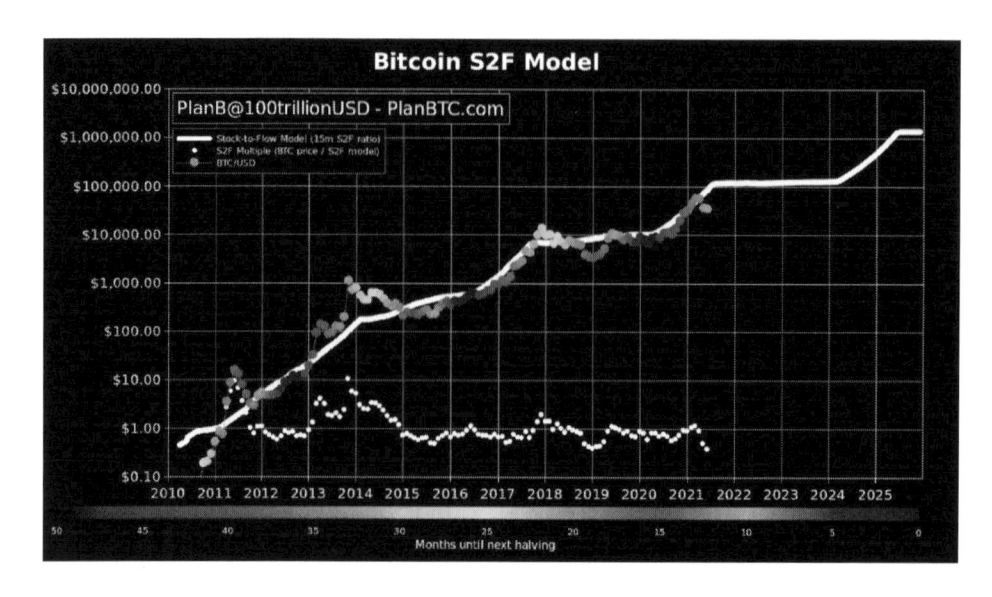

The white line is the price prediction and the color dotted line is the actual price.

As we can see, the price goes up in steps due to the process known as "halvings" where the daily supply of BTC gets cut by half every 4 years. This produces a squeeze in the supply that pushes the price up.

21 million is a very small amount in a world where there are 50 million millionaires, 1000+ publicly traded companies, and a population of 8 billion. Very few people will be able to own even half BTC in the future.

Most people think it's too late now, that they should have bought at $100 when they had the chance, but this is far from the truth. Bitcoin always seems expensive when looking back but cheap when looking forward. Those who are able to buy below $100,000 are getting a great deal and will be able to multiply their money by 10x at least.

Of course, nobody knows the future, something could go wrong and end up this venture overnight, but the probabilities of BTC going to a million are much higher than it going to zero.

Store of Value

Some investors are not so interested in increasing their wealth as much as retaining purchasing power. They look for alternatives in assets that appreciate at least as much as inflation.

Tradicional investment vehicles used as hedges are gold, real estate, art, and the stock market. All of these come with their own flaws.

Gold has been stagnant for years. Real estate is illiquid and messy. The stock market is slow and unreliable at best. Art could be a good option if chosen carefully.

But bitcoin is a superior asset class. It appreciates 200% a year, is scarce, secure, easy to buy and hodl and unseizable. Investors are beginning to realize this and getting some exposure to the crypto asset.

Even taking into account the volatility, BTC is by far the best store of value out there. Over a 5 year period, its performance is unbeatable.

Hedge against inflation

Unlike Fiat, bitcoin is deflationary, meaning its value goes up instead of down like the Bolivar, the Peso, or even the Dollar.

In inflationary scenarios, like the current one, it's the perfect vehicle to protect your wealth. Bitcoin is actually replacing gold as an inflation hedge due to its superior qualities.

Insurance against confiscation

Once you put your Bitcoin in a cold wallet and store it in a safe place, no one can take it from you. Not the government, not the FBI, not the North Korean hackers, and not China.

No other asset has this level of security. Your money in the bank, your house, and even your gold can be taken away from you by decree. You can always fight it in court but good luck with that.

Confiscation doesn't happen that often in the first world, but the possibility is always there. The US confiscated all gold from its citizens in 1931 and it was never returned to its rightful owners.

But in developing countries, they know this all too well. Most people in Latin America hide their money under the mattress because they don't trust banks or the government.

Bitcoin is trustless technology. Don trust, verify is the motto here.

Who can benefit from bitcoin?

Well, just about everyone, but surprisingly the poor more than the rich.

Bitcoin for the poor

Bitcoin is not a toy for rich kids as we have been led to believe. Bitcoin is particularly useful for those who have lived under oppressive monetary systems which account for a big chunk of the world's population.

In this day and age, 2 billion people are still unbanked. We complain a lot about banks, but imagine not having access to a safe place to park your money, no credit facilities, and no investment vehicles.

On top of that, another 4 billion are underbanked with very limited services and extortionate fees.

Fortunately, these 6 billion people now have hope. They can access the biggest bank in the world from their phone. They don't need permission, credentials, or IDs. They don't have to put up with hyperinflation, devaluation, or confiscation. No one is going to block their account for their ideology, gender, religion, or race.

Bitcoin opens the floodgates to 70% of the planet and they can now have hope for the future.

People in the first world with credit cards, bank accounts, and investment options, find it harder to accept the concept of a decentralized currency. But the moment you tell someone from Venezuela, Argentina, Sudan, or Nigeria, they immediately understand the benefits.

Money that doesn't suffer from inflation, confiscation, or censorship is a big deal in many places around the world. On top of that, with crypto, they have access to small credits and they can even lend money to others on a peer-to-peer basis.

As Michael Saylor says, **money is energy**, and you need a proper place to store it securely, otherways it gets lost.

The right to own property is one of the basic human needs, without it there is no freedom, dignity, or hope. If you don't agree with this statement, go visit Venezuela, Zimbabwe, or North Korea and see for yourself.

All the attempts to eliminate poverty will fail until people have a proper vehicle to preserve their wealth. Now, 6 billion people have the opportunity to improve their lives from a wallet in their phone.

Bitcoin fixes this

Anyone with internet access can download an app, buy some crypto and start using the services provided by DeFi. From this wallet, borrowing, lending, saving, investing, and doing payments is possible.

This technology could achieve what the UN, UNICEF, the IMF, and the World Bank have failed at; improving the lives of millions in a sustainable way.

El Salvador

In El Zonte beach, a community of bitcoin enthusiasts has been running an experiment for years. Every shop, restaurant, or service accepts bitcoin as payment. This project has worked so well that president Bukele has decided to make it legal tender in the whole country.

This is the first time in history a country adopts a decentralized currency they have no control over.

This is a risky move but there are many reasons to believe it will pay off. For starters, they get rid of inflation which is already a nice bonus.

Besides, 70% of the population in El Salvador is unbanked and now can have a bank in their pocket.

And to top it up, they rely heavily on remittances sent from abroad. Intermediaries like Western Union and MoneyCorp charge hefty commissions that now will be reduced to almost zero by the use of bitcoin and the Lightning Network.

Now, anyone from anywhere can send money in seconds and at almost zero cost.

Since the president made this announcement the economy in this small country on the pacific coast is booming. GDP is expected to grow substantially, entrepreneurs and investors are moving in and even the tourism industry is benefiting from this trend.

Some people think this is a risky move but I don't think so. What do they have to lose anyway? El Salvador has been hit by violence, poverty, corruption, and inflation forever. Now with bitcoin, all this could change for the better.

In order to increase adoption, the government decided in September to give away $30 worth of bitcoin to any Salvadorian who opened a Chivo wallet account. As of today (Oct,18th, 2021), that money has appreciated in value 50%. Needless to say, people are delighted that for the first time in history, their currency is going up in value instead of down.
So far, 3 million people (50% of the population) have signed up for the crypto wallet. Now, the number of people using crypto is higher than that using banks.

To top it all up, there is plenty of geothermal energy in the country coming from volcanoes. This is currently being used to mine bitcoin at a low price. It's a match made in heaven.

Venezuela

A few years ago I visited Venezuela, the price of a beer was just a few Bolivars. Now the same beer costs several million.

Money in Venezuela is worthless, so it's not surprising that Bitcoin adoption is one of the highest in the world. People gravitate toward hard money, a currency that doesn't lose value and an asset that appreciates instead of depreciating.

Even the dollar is inflating faster than ever and it's fast losing its status as a safe haven against inflation.

Besides, bitcoin is censorship-resistant, unseizable, and permissionless. All you need is a phone, no bank account required. This makes it the perfect vehicle for countries where property rights, are not respected.

Soon, the Bolivar will disappear and the whole country will join the bitcoinazation revolution.

Argentina

In 2002, during a financial crisis known as "El Corralito", the Argentinian government decided to freeze all bank accounts, devalue the currency 100:1, and force the exchange from dollars to pesos at a very low rate.

Basically, people lost 90% of their money and this includes the dollars deposited in bank accounts.

This will never happen again. Argentinians have learned the lesson. Now, they have bitcoin. No government can ever confiscate, devalue or censor bitcoin even if they try.

What would you do if your country decided to do "a corralito"? Is your money safe? Are you sure?

You might think this only happens in Latin America but the reality might be very different. Governments all over the world are getting desperate and they have the power to seize any funds by any means they might deem necessary.

Let's hope it doesn't get to that, but if it does, are you prepared for it?

Traditionally, people have used gold as a hedge but gold is very easily confiscable. It normally lives in banks' vaults so they are in control. Even if you hide it under the mattress, you won't be able to take it with you if you have to emigrate.

But remember, the time to get ready is now, not later. When the proverbial Shit Hits The Fan, it'll be too late.

Investments

All my life, I've been looking for a way to park my money with decent returns. I've tried everything out there but the results have been unsatisfactory. I wasn't looking for a quick way to make a bug, I just wanted to avoid inflation.

The stock market can be stagnant for years and then all of a sudden it shoots through the roof.

Real estate is a hassle, illiquid, and with lots of hidden costs and taxes.

Gold is dead. It's been producing negative yields for the last 10 years.

Bitcoin. Appreciates 200% a year on average and it's easy to buy, hold and secure. It's also very liquid.

Obviously, bitcoin has some risks but so do all the other investments. Taking into account the risk/benefit ratio we have a clear winner.

Here's a comparison between the compound return for bitcoin, gold, and the S&P 500 for the last 10 years:

Bitcoin & Traditional Assets ROI (vs USD)

	Bitcoin	Gold	S&P 500
1 year:	+280%	-17%	+32%
2 year:	+271%	+12%	+52%
3 year:	+591%	+39%	+55%
4 year:	+1,210%	+32%	+81%
5 year:	+7,459%	+26%	+103%
6 year:	+16,418%	+53%	+112%
7 year:	+7,494%	+30%	+131%
8 year:	+47,056%	+29%	+162%
9 year:	+384,344%	+5%	+215%
10 year:	+469,482%	-3%	+286%

Diversification

I often hear investors recommending having a diversified portfolio; don't put all your eggs in one basket and all that. This is all very well and good, but when you have a clear winner why not go 100% in?

Would you diversify into Blackberry, Blockbuster, or Kodak? No, you wouldn't because these were losing propositions and it was obvious they were doomed the moment they were disrupted by technology.

For the same reason, you should not diversify into a sinking titanic and you should not put your money in banks or Fiat money. These are the new Internet explorers of our time.

Diversifying sounds like a good idea but it will make you lose 90% of your money.

I think only technology companies, some real estate, and some crypto assets are worth it. The rest is very risky. Of these three, bitcoin is the easiest and the safest.

After the advent of the internet, did you put money in books, music, maps, or movies?

After Amazon's success, would you invest in retail?

Diversifying is fine when there is no clear trend, not enough information or the outcome is unpredictable. But betting against a technology whose time has come is financial suicide.

Taking the time to study the markets, the technology, and the trends is a much safer bet than just blind shooting in the hope that one bullet might hit the target.

Warren Buffet doesn't diversify, he studies companies and industries for years and then goes all in. It has definitely worked nicely for him.

Be careful where you put your money, bitcoin is the nemesis for banks, Fiat money, and Wall Street.

Bull market

Right now (Oct 2021) we are in the middle of a bull market that will last until mid-2022 or probably longer. All these ups and downs and volatility are just noise. Year on year, bitcoin has produced returns of 250% at the time of writing.

Despite the doomsayers, the FUD, and the negative narrative, bitcoin keeps reaching higher highs and higher lows. It's a scarce asset with limited supply and unlimited demand, the sky's the limit.

Bull markets are usually triggered by the halvings - the reduction of daily supply done every 4 years. In 2020 we had the last halving and the daily flow of bitcoin went from 1800 to 900. In 2024, it will go down to 450 and so on. This has been the main trigger of bull markets.

But this time, things might be different. Never before have we seen so much institutional adoption, funds, ETFs, and big investors joining in. Some experts forecast that we'll move into a supercycle that will last forever due to the shrinking supply and the ever-growing demand.

So far, BTC's performance has been impeccable, no other asset in history has appreciated so much and so fast. It took gold 5000 years to achieve these levels but, for bitcoin, it only took 12 years.

Let's see why bitcoin offers many advantages over legacy systems.

Chapter 4

Bitcoin as a lifeboat

Bitcoin is a safe haven. Satoshi Nakamoto's motivation was to provide an alternative to the Fiat money system and the questionable practices of banks and Wall Street. The last straw in the camel's back was the second bailout for banks in 2008. Nakamoto posted this frontpage on a message site:

Understandably, Satoshi was outraged by the privatization of profits and the socialization of losses done by banks and governments and this is precisely what Bitcoin aims to stop.

Bitcoin offers an alternative to this opaque, corrupt, and obsolete system of inflation, devaluation, and unlimited printing.

These are some of the problems bitcoin fixes.

Inflation

With all this money printing and quantitative easing, inflation is inevitable. The dollar supply has increased 40% in the last 12 months and this is only the beginning.

The government has admitted that Consumer Price Index is on the rise but they are embellishing the figures. According to some independent studies like the Shadow Government Statistics, we are already at 10% inflation at least and it's likely to hit 20 % in the near future.

If this is correct, your money will be halved in 5 years unless you do something about it. The dollar, that is regarded as the strongest currency, is not as strong as we might think. It has lost 98% of its value in the last 100 years.

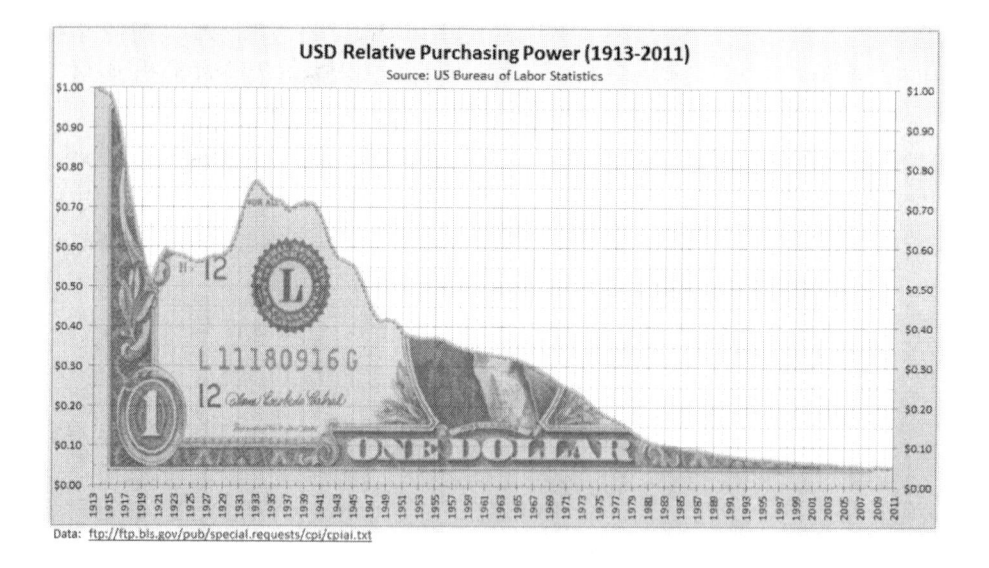

USD Relative Purchasing Power (1913-2011)
Source: US Bureau of Labor Statistics

Data: ftp://ftp.bls.gov/pub/special.requests/cpi/cpiai.txt

If this has happened to the world's reserve currency, imagine what happened to the rest.

Increasing supply is generally a bad idea, it debases the currency and encourages governments to get into debt and hypothecate the future. An extreme example of this is Venezuela, but this is happening on a global scale.

Bitcoin is a hedge against money printing, inflation, and debt. Even seasoned investors like Ray Dalio recommend having some exposure to crypto in a balanced portfolio.

The Antidote

One of Bitcoin's strong selling points is scarcity. The total supply is capped at 21 million of which, 18.8 million are already in circulation.

But it gets even better. Of those 21 million, between 4 to 7 million have been lost forever - forgotten passwords, deceased owners, faulty equipment, etc. Let's keep in mind that in the past it was very easy and cheap to mine bitcoin so people didn't secure them properly and old equipment got thrown away.

For instance, Nakamoto's wallet contains over a million BTC and he/she is probably dead. No one will ever be able to access it, not the CIA, not the FBI, not China, and not North Korean hackers. This is how safe the system is.

This means that bitcoin is more scarce than originally thought, and it's likely that there are only about 16 million to go around.

In a world with 50 million millionaires, 1000 publicly traded companies, 180 countries, and 8 billion people, when even a tiny percentage of them decide to join the party, the supply squeeze will push the price through the roof.

While most fiat currencies remain inflationary, bitcoin is deflationary and it can act as a buffer protecting economies from inflation bubbles.

Confiscation

Confiscation doesn't just happen in Argentina. In 1933, the US government decided to confiscate all gold from its citizens, never to be returned. A new law is all it takes to get hold of your assets and make them disappear forever. You can always fight it in court, but good luck with that.

I remember in the 80s, the Spanish government decided to nationalize Rumasa, a big industrial and commercial business conglomerate. Just like that, the rightful owner and his company parted forever and there was nothing he could do about it.

After several years in court, the owner got some compensation but never really recovered his empire. Keep in mind, this was done in a democratic, stable country that follows the rule of law and the right to own property.

Basically, everything you think you own is not really yours, it belongs to the state, and when they claim it back, there is nothing you can do.

Unless…

…you own bitcoin. Bitcoin is unseizable. When you put it in a secure place, no one knows you have it and no one can take it away from you. It's not like we all should be wearing tin foil hats but, on the other hand, can we really trust the government?

Banks

Banks are in deep trouble. On one hand, they have unwelcomed competition from bitcoin and DeFi, on the other hand, Central Bank Digital Currencies (CBDCs) are coming fast.

Bitcoin and DeFi protocols offer more security, better services, fewer fees, and more speed than banks could ever achieve. It's just a superior technology and the legacy industry just can't compete.

In 10 years, the banking industry will be decimated so now it's time to look for alternatives before it's too late. In the past, we had horses and buggies, now we have cars. In the future, we'll have electric autonomous cars. Following this natural progression, banks will soon be replaced by bitcoin.

With bitcoin, you can save, invest, borrow and lend. All with better rates. Celsius, a lending platform, offers 12% interest on deposits and 1% on loans.

As investments go, no one can compete with BTC. All those funds, pensions, and deposits offered by banks pale in comparison to crypto returns.

With bitcoin, your bank is in your pocket.

CBDCs

In response to Bitcoin, central banks are reacting to bitcoin by creating their own digital currencies. These currencies will be centralized, inflationary and 100% manipulable.

This by itself, will make banks obsolete. The main purpose of commercial banks is to act as intermediaries between the money supply and the final customers.

When CBDC's are in place, money will flow directly from the FED to your phone, leapfrogging the banking industry. This way central banks will gain even more control and will be better positioned to compete with bitcoin.

But CBDCs are not good news for us. Such currencies will be used as tools to spy and control citizens. They will know exactly where you spend your money and can stop you from doing so if they deem it necessary.

If you are a smoker, they can block you from buying tobacco, if you drink the same, if you buy meat they can argue it's not good for the planet, and so on.

The moment you accept CBDCs, you give all independence and sovereignty to big brother and you'll never get it back.

They won't allow you to buy bitcoin either, of course. So you either buy it now or get trapped in that Orwellian dystopia forever.

Insurance

Bitcoin is not just an investment, it's a safe haven. When the systems we have in place start collapsing, when institutions can no longer be trusted, when the world around you starts looking unstable, don't worry, you have a lifeboat.

Bitcoin is protection against power structures that have been wronging us for years and are about to be dismantled.

Bitcoin now is like the internet in the 90s, you either join the party or you'll be left behind.

Don't let fear dictate your life. Make the decision with better odds of success. It's very risky to bet against technology.

A friend of mine from Venezuela was worried about Chavez getting to power in the late 90s. He had a nice house, a nice car, and a good middle-class lifestyle in general. I told him to sell everything and leave the country. He kind of agreed with me but never took the plunge. Now, he and his family are struggling to survive.

It's not that hard to see patterns if you look close enough. Often we are blinded by fear and hesitation but still, it's possible to see certain trends emerging that offer clues about where we are heading.

If you think the world is changing beyond recognition in the next few years, you should act now. If you don't, you need better glasses. Don't be paralyzed by fear like my friend or you'll live a life of regret.

Bitcoin is your life insurance.

Wake up

Bitcoin is a safe haven in times of uncertainty. We are now in the middle of the biggest economic crisis in history caused by COVID-19. The perfect storm is brewing and bitcoin is one of the few lifeboats.

Inflation, unemployment, the pandemic, the collapse of many industries, and CBDCs are going to make the world a dangerous place. You can carry on, as usual, doing your job, watching Netflix, and burying your head in the sand or you can wake up and get ready for the tsunami. Up to you.

Chapter 5

Bitcoin vs Fiat

Bitcoin is superior to Fiat money, at least in certain aspects. These are some of the most relevant.

Store of value

Fiat money keeps devaluing fast while BTC keeps appreciating at 200% a year. Nobody regards the Dollar or the Euro as a good place to park cash anymore.

Traditionally, other assets like gold or property have been used as protection against inflation. But these assets are cumbersome and not so great investments compared to bitcoin.

Bitcoin is a pristine asset, with high liquidity, great performance, and tamper-proof security. The world is waking up to this fact and abandoning traditional investment vehicles like gold, silver, and even stocks.

Bitcoin has appreciated 6,000,000% in 10 years and it's still cheap according to most experts. If you want to leave a legacy for your children, there is nothing better out there.

Unit of account

We often use the dollar or the Euro to measure value, i.e. a house costs $500,000, a car $50,000, and a coffee $5.

But due to money printing and inflation, prices keep going up and the value of money keeps going down.

Lately, we've seen real estate prices going up by 20% in some areas, but this increase is actually deceiving. It's actually the dollar going down and not the other way round.

With bitcoin, the opposite is true. A house that used to cost 10,000 BTC now costs 10 BTC. Eventually, bitcoin will stabilize, and then it'll become a better reference to measure value than all those depreciating currencies.

Another example. The Caracas stock exchange has gone up 4,100,000,000% in the last 20 years. This is quite impressive, right? Not quite. That's only when measured in Bolivars, when measured in dollars, its value is actually near zero. This is why it's important to use the right unit of account.

Medium of exchange

One of the main uses of money is the ability to buy stuff with it.

Bitcoin is also a medium of exchange and it's also natively digital making it more suitable for the online world.

Bitcoin is truly global, divisible up to 100 million, and 100% digital. Anyone with a phone can use it to pay or receive payments. In comparison, the dollar is much less convenient when used as a global currency.

International currency

Forget about exchanging currencies every time you cross borders thus losing a lot of money in fees. With bitcoin, you can pay in most establishments without the need to handle any dirty notes.

El Salvador has been a pioneer in bitcoin adoption but this will soon be spreading to many touristy locations. It's a win-win situation for tourists and vendors and it was about time we had something like this.

One of the main advantages of adopting the Euro was the ability to travel within the Eurozone without having to convert money. I remember thinking this was very convenient and wished it could be extended to more countries. Now it has.

El Zonte

In El Zonte Beach is possible to pay just about everything with bitcoin. This small scale experiment has been running for years with great success. Tourism is booming and the locals are happy to be dealing with a proper currency that's easy to use and has many advantages over Fiat money.

The New Gold

In 1971, the gold standard was abandoned and Fiat money became the norm. This has been regarded by many as a mistake. After all, gold is a hard asset, with limited supply and a predictable flow.

But everything comes to an end. Gold reign is being undermined by this new asset class and there are many doubts about its future.

A few years ago, 1 ounce of gold was 8000 BTC, now it's 0.02 BTC. This shows the decline of the once world's favorite asset when compared to the new kid on the block.

Gold is on its way out. It might retain some value due to its ornamental, jewelry, and industrial uses but it can't compete in the digital era.

$1.6 billion in gold vs bitcoin. Which one do you think is the future?

Backing up the Dollar

Up until 1971, the dollar was based on the gold standard by which the FED could only issue a limited amount of dollars proportional to the gold reserves.

This made the dollar a solid asset, a hard currency, and sound money. However, ever since the dollar became Fiat, it became a soft currency and lost most of its value.

It could be argued that for money to be real, it needs to have some limits, some constraints. You can't just print infinite money and then pretend it'll hold its value.

Although the dollar has debased by 98%, it is still the strongest Fiat currency out there. However, if it wants to remain relevant in the 21st century it will need some support, some backing.

The dollar can't compete with bitcoin for many reasons but it could find support in it. I believe the only chance the dollar has to survive is to join the bitcoin standard and be supported by the cryptocurrency. The dollar was stronger when it was backed by gold, and now bitcoin could be the new support for the green bill.

Remittances

Every year, $1 Trillion is sent around the world from relatives to help their families in poor countries. Companies like Western Union make a fortune on commissions that amount up to 40% in some cases.

With bitcoin, you can send money between wallets, with no intermediaries, in seconds and at zero cost.

This is going to revolutionize the remittances market, saving millions that traditionally get lost in the way.

Bitcoin as legal tender

El Salvador is the first country in the world to adopt bitcoin as legal tender. Many other countries will follow suit. This makes a lot of sense in economies with weak currencies that struggle with inflation, devaluation, and instability.

Argentina, Paraguay, Panama, Brazil, and others are already discussing it but many more are unofficially adopting it. Venezuela, Nigeria, and Vietnam are pretty much-bitcoin-based economies already.

Sovereign reserve

Countries could soon start buying Bitcoin and keep it as a reserve currency like they used to do with gold. It makes sense and some are probably already doing it discreetly.

Chapter 6

Decentralized systems

Decentralization

Bitcoin is the most distributed network out there. With thousands of nodes and miners and millions of wallets, there is no other system that offers the same amount of decentralization.

Recently, China decided to ban mining in its territory. That was a huge blow for Bitcoin considering 80% of mining was done within its borders. Within a few days, the miners started relocating to other countries and the bitcoin operation recovered rather quickly.

No other network would have survived such disruption without going down.

These are some of the benefits of decentralization.

Transportable

Just by remembering a 24-word seed phrase you can go anywhere in the world and carry your money with you. No one can stop you or confiscate it. Try doing that with gold.

Permissionless

To open a bank account, to transfer money, to invest, to buy stocks, or to buy gold, you need permission.

Not with bitcoin.

No gatekeeper can keep you from entering the crypto world. This system allows financial access to millions who are unbanked, making the system more egalitarian and democratic than any other financial institution before.

Censorship resistant

Unfortunately, there are still many countries where basic human rights are not respected by the authorities. One of the most powerful tools for oppressors is canceling people's access to money.

When they freeze your bank account, confiscate your assets, or simply stop you from spending, it is not much you can do to defend yourself.

But they can't take away bitcoin. Owning BTC allows people to regain some freedom and give them options to defend themselves against tyranny and oppression.

Transparent

Bitcoin is pseudo-anonymous, all transactions can be seen in the public blockchain but it's not easy to identify the person or company behind them.

Big wallets are easier to track since their volumes are more conspicuous. For example, there is only 1 wallet with 1 million BTCs and it belongs to Satoshi Nakamoto. But for the millions of wallets holding 0.1 BTC, it is almost impossible to identify the owner unless there is a specific reason and the FBI decides to investigate.

In the on-chain platform glassnode.com, anyone can look up blockchain addresses and transactions in real-time.

Conversely, on Wall Street, most transactions are done behind closed doors with insider trading and opaque operations being the norm.

Bitcoin is open, transparent, and immutable and it brings a breath of fresh air to a crony, obsolete financial system designed by politicians and bankers.

Immutable

Every transaction gets recorded in the blockchain forever in an immutable way. Your bank could manipulate the data in your account but not in the blockchain. This guarantees the integrity of the process and reinforces trust in the system.

DeFi

Decentralized Finance creates a world of opportunities for investors and traders. Here are some of the possibilities:

- Yield farming. This a way to invest in coin or token projects at an early stage with a high yield but with high risk also
- Liquidity pool. New tokens need liquidity and the providers can have a handsome return. Some offer up to 1200% interest. Again this is risky unless you know what you are doing

- Stablecoins. Coins pegged to the dollar serve as a bridge between the crypto and the Fiat world. Typical yields are 6-19%
- Lending. Platforms like Celsius or BlockFi offer generous returns to those who are willing to lend their crypto to others
- Loan platforms. You can also borrow money for as low as 1%
- NFTs. Digital signatures make digital art, music, or video unique and in some cases increase their value exponentially

This ecosystem evolves rapidly and creates new opportunities for investment, careers, or business. It is worth keeping an eye on it and studying the trends of this exciting new technology.

Coins vs Tokens

These two terms are often used interchangeably but are in fact, two different concepts.

A coin is a crypto asset that runs on its own blockchain while a token runs on third-party solutions.

Examples of coins are Bitcoin, Ethereum, and Binance coin. Examples of tokens are Bitcoin cash, Basic Attention Token, and BUSD.

The Ethereum platform is called ERC-20 and is by far the most popular base for other tokens to run.

Layer 2 solutions

Most coins use layer 1 where the blockchain, the protocol, and the network reside. This is the most secure, and reliable layer but it can be slow and expensive at times.

For small transactions, like paying for a coffee, there is a layer 2 solution. Bitcoin's layer 2 is called the Lighting network and allows for faster payments and very low fees permitting the use of bitcoin as a day-to-day currency.

Ethereum also suffers from bottlenecks in layer 1 but in order to correct this, it's migrating to a Proof of Stake system which is faster and cheaper. This has been a big selling point for ETH but BTC is catching up fast with the introduction of the Lighting network.

Proof of Work

Bitcoin and Ethereum (so far) are based on the PoW protocol to ensure the integrity of the operation.

Miners compete to solve mathematical puzzles in order to achieve a block reward every 10 mins and earn either 6.25 BTC or 5 ETH respectively.

PoW consumes time and energy but ensures the transactions are irreversible and secure. Once an entry has been verified in the blockchain, it is almost impossible to reverse it, making the system very reliable.

PoW can be slow and expensive but this is done by design, it's a feature, not a bug. PoW is what makes bitcoin the safest asset out there.

Proof of Stake (PoS)

Ethereum is migrating to PoS to make faster and cheaper transactions. There is an ongoing debate about this and some critics regard PoS as a mistake because it could make the network more centralized and insecure. Only time will tell.

PoS implements a system of voting in which the biggest stakers decide how to settle discrepancies. It makes the system more efficient but somehow less democratic. Advocates of PoS defend it arguing that it's worth sacrificing some centralization in order to provide a better service.

ETH 2.0 is about one year away so it'll be interesting to see how things evolve in this arena.

Satoshis

Bitcoin is appreciating so fast that soon it'll be too big to handle as a unit of account. This was predicted by Nakamoto and the solution is to use fractional units called Satoshis.

1BTC = 100,000,000 Sats

Right now $1 = 1600 Sats but soon will probably be much less as BTC appreciates.

Satoshi will become the preferred unit of account for small transactions.

Central Bank Digital Currencies (CBDCs)

In order to survive, central banks are being forced to mint their own digital currencies so they can compete with bitcoin.

CBDCs are, however, very different from decentralized crypto. Central banks have total power over these currencies and they can manipulate them at will.

CBDCs are tools to spy and control citizens. With them, governments know where you spend your money and will be able to stop you from doing so. They can also freeze or seize your funds for any reason they deem necessary.

For example, let's say you want to buy meat but your government doesn't recommend it. At check out the transaction gets rejected and unless you have another currency, you won't be able to buy the item.

CBDCs are a dangerous weapon, the problem is that governments can force their adoption by paying salaries, pensions and collecting taxes, fees, and fines in it.

CBDCs are created in a central database and distributed directly to each citizen's wallet, doing away with the need for middlemen.

In China, they even put an expiration date on money to force people to spend it fast.

This is an Orwellian dystopia that we'll see very soon in Europe and the US. The only way to escape is by moving into crypto asap. Once CBDCs are in place they will limit the purchase of BTC since they don't welcome competition. It could become 1984.

Chapter 7

Urban legends and FUD

FUD

Fear, Uncertainty, and Doubt. This is the acronym for FUD that is often used by the media and politicians to attack anything they don't understand.

Bitcoin is a disruptive technology and therefore is not easy to grasp, especially because we are used to legacy systems like Fiat money and banking services.

FUD comes from misunderstanding the technology but also some ill-intentioned agendas.

Horse breeders spread a lot of FUD when the automobile was taking off. They were scared and quite rightly so. The same is happening now with crypto.

Now, governments and banks are afraid of losing control and privileges but all they can do is to spread lies about it in the hope to confuse the public.

Every time you hear an attack on Bitcoin ask yourself: What's the agenda behind this person or institution? Do they really believe what they say or are they just worried by the threat of something better?

The Internet in the 90s caused a lot of FUD also - *it wastes electricity, it's slow, it's just for criminals, it's expensive, etc.* Does this sound familiar?

Bitcoin is a powerful technology and it has created multiple enemies. This is some of the common FUD they are spreading:

- It's a scam
- It's only for criminals
- It boils the oceans
- It's a Ponzi scheme
- It's too volatile
- It's pure speculation

All these accusations have been proved wrong over and over again.

Bitcoin haters are a bit desperate and don't know what fake news to make up anymore.

Let's have a look at every objection they've presented so far.

Volatility

Bitcoin is volatile, sure, but volatility is the price to pay for something that appreciates 200% a year. Gold was volatile 100 years ago and then it became stable. Bitcoin is following the same path.

Besides, what do you prefer? An asset that goes up 200% and then down 50% or one that always goes down in value like the dollar?

Volatility is a feature, not a flaw.

Money for criminals

Bitcoin has been used for illegal activities - the silk road and all that. But then, criminals realized that the blockchain is transparent and immutable so they stopped using it.

Only a tiny fraction of illegal activities are done using crypto while this number goes to 98% with dollars. Cash is the only form of anonymous money, that's why it's still preferred by criminals.

Global warming

Bitcoin uses electricity, about 0.1% of the world's supply to be precise. However, more than 50% comes from renewables. Another big chunk comes from stranded energy that would be wasted anyway and this ratio keeps growing. In a few years, all the mining will be done with green energy.

Besides, Bitcoin is much greener than all the industries and assets it is trying to replace - Fiat money, banking, financial services, etc.

And on top of that, bitcoin is promoting the construction of green power plants by buying all their energy on the spot.

Thanks to bitcoin, the planet will be greener and not the other way around.

It's a Ponzi Scheme

No Ponzi scheme lasts for 12 years, gets to $1 Trillion by market cap, and attracts big institutions like Tesla, Microstrategy, or Grayscale.

Even Ray Dalio recommends it.

Was the internet a Ponzi scheme? What about Google, Apple, or Amazon?

People that accuse bitcoin of being a Ponzi scheme don't understand either.

It's too centralized in China

This FUD has been going on for years until China got rid of most miners. Now, they can't use it anymore.

Bitcoin is the most decentralized network ever invented. Even if 80% of the nodes were attacked, the system will stay up functioning properly with the other 20%. Bitcoin is antifragile and unsinkable.

Not even China can destroy Bitcoin.

It's pure speculation

If you only look at the price, you could be forgiven for thinking it is just a speculative asset. However, if you look at the fundamentals, you'll realize it is not.

The blockchain, Proof of Work, the consensus mechanism, the protocol, the encryption, and the scarcity make bitcoin a pristine asset and state-of-the-art technology.

Nakamoto is a genius in Math, cryptography, IT, and economics, and bitcoin is the pinnacle of human invention.

It has solved problems that remained unsolved for centuries like how to make transactions between parties without the need for trust, how to solve the Byzantine Generals problem, how to fix the double-spending problem, and how to make a digital asset uncopyable.

All these are real solutions to real problems humanity has had for centuries. Now, thanks to bitcoin, they've been solved forever.

Bitcoin is a lot more than just a speculative asset.

Chapter 8

Altcoins

Fiat money is no match for bitcoin but how about all the other cryptocurrencies out there?

Well, it depends. If you ask bitcoin maximalists, they will tell you to stay away from any other coin and they actually have a point.

However, there are some use cases in which Altcoins might come handy. Some are good for tokenization, others for smart contracts, and others for social media, sports, or specific applications.

But as a monetary technology, nothing can compare to bitcoin. Just the scarcity, the Proof of Work mechanism, and the Network make bitcoin the best financial asset ever created. If you only buy one coin make sure it's bitcoin. Also, I would recommend putting at least 50% of your portfolio in bitcoin. (Not financial advice)

Bitcoin is superior to other alternatives for 3 main reasons:

- the network effect
- the first-mover advantage
- the true decentralization

The network effect

According to Metcalfe's law, a network's value is proportional to the square of the number of nodes in the network.

Bitcoin has 40,000 nodes and keeps growing. This makes it unreachable by other networks making the system very robust.

The runner-up, Ethereum, has 11,000 nodes which is impressive, but it won't be able to catch up anytime soon.

The network effect can be understood better by studying other businesses. What does Coca-cola, Macdonald's, or the US domestic electrical network have in common?

All these are easily copied and improved, however, it's very unlikely any competitor will ever overtake them due to the network effects.

Making a sugary drink better than coke is easy, yet, can they emulate their distribution network?

Making a better burger than Mcdonalds is simple, however, opening thousands of fast food venues all over the world is just not feasible.

110v electricity outlets in the American household are obsolete, yet, who is going to change the whole infrastructure for millions of homes?

Network effects are very powerful. Once a system is in place and has reached a critical number of nodes, it'll most probably stay there forever.

Bitcoin is not the fastest, the cheapest, or the most efficient. In fact, it only does one thing well - storing value - but this does it like no other.

All these bitcoin killers will never have the network, the miners, the nodes, the coders or the users bitcoin has. Besides, many altcoins are trying to do too many things at once and this lack of focus will be their demise.

The likelihood of any coin flippening bitcoin is almost zero.

However, there are some coins with interesting use cases.

Let's see some of the ones I like.

Ethereum (ETH)

Although Bitcoin is also programmable money, ethereum is specifically designed for this purpose. ETH programming language is called Solidity and it runs applications like Smart Contracts, Decentralized Apps, DAOs, NFTs.

These apps have multiple applications and Ethereum is very well positioned to take over these markets.
Decentralized Finance (DeFi) has the potential to steal market share from Wall Street, trading, and financial intermediaries. This is a multi Trillion market industry and Ethereum is the main candidate to run the show.

With DeFi, transactions are transparent, irreversible, fast, and cheap, no middlemen are required and the system is open 24/7. DeFi could inflict a lot of damage in the crony, opaque, and obsolete world of finance.

Smart Contracts could replace traditional contracts and do away with the need for lawyers, endless negotiations, and final settlements.

Ethereum is the ideal platform for all these Apps and this adds a lot of value to the network.

Besides, the Ethereum protocol (ERC-20) is the base for many other tokens like USDC thus benefiting from second-order effects.

ChainLink, Compound, Synthetix, Maker, Tron, Uniswap, and Tether are some of the projects that run under the ERC-20 protocol. These are excellent projects with lots of potential that will take off and push ETH price even higher.

Besides, Ethereum is migrating from Proof of Work to Proof of Stake and this will make for cheaper and faster transactions. Some critics say this will bring some vulnerabilities to the system but this remains to be seen.

Binance Coin (BNB)

Binance is the biggest exchange in the crypto sphere and they have their own coin.

Just because of the huge number of customers, BNB has a lot of potential and high growth is to be expected.

However, BNB is not decentralized so it might present some vulnerabilities in the future. Decentralization in crypto is the holy grail although some projects have chosen to go against the tide in order to improve efficiency and control.

Polygon (Matic)

Polygon is a token that runs under the ERC-20 protocol and offers scalability and structural development. Polygon serves as a bridge between ETH and other blockchains facilitating interoperability.

This could potentially be a great feature since there are many blockchains trying to speak to each other.

The threat for Polygon could come with the implementation of ETH2.0 which could reduce its use cases. But even with this possibility in mind, it has a promising future.

Solana (SOL)

Solana uses the proof of History protocol which provides the platform with scalability, utility, and speed at a very low cost.

It has big institutional support and its potential for appreciation is quite high.

Chainlink (LINK)

ChainLink is an oracle that provides interoperability between different platforms. Besides, it specializes in off-chain data for smart contracts.

Cardano (ADA)

Allegedly, the Ethereum killer although so far it's not been able to live up to the expectations.

ADA's biggest selling point is to become Africa's currency. If they manage to achieve this, the price could go exponential. Worth keeping an eye on.

Some other projects I like

Algorand, Compound, 1Inch, Zilliqa, Enjin, Chilliz, Avalanche, and AAVE are solid projects with strong fundamentals that could explode soon.

Risk

Altcoins tend to go up faster than bitcoin but then also drop faster.

Right now, we are in the middle of a bull market and everything is effervescent but when the music stops, it's much safer to put your money in bitcoin, ETH, or some stablecoins.

A common strategy I use and recommend is the 50-25-25. 50% Bitcoin, 25% ETH and the rest Altcoins.

DeFi

Decentralized Finance is a very promising technology that could disrupt the traditional financial system.

Up until now, all transactions are handled by centralized systems - banks, brokers, financial institutions, etc. These organizations are managed by people who are fallible, inefficient, and often corrupt.

Wall Street, for example, is open 8 to 3, Monday to Friday. DeFi is open 24/7 365. In this time and age, people don't like to wait for 3 days to clear a transaction.

Crypto Exchanges could be Centralized (CEX), like Kraken, Coinbase, and Binance, or Decentralized (DEX) like UniSwap, PanCakeSwap, and Compound.

DEXs are peer-to-peer platforms where people and Bots meet to trade tokens. No intermediary is required.

DEXs are more difficult to use and are still experiencing teething problems but once they mature, most transactions will be done through them. DEX is the future of finance.

DEXs are riskier in general and not advisable for beginners but once you familiarize yourself with this ecosystem, it opens new possibilities that are not available through the traditional channels.

Stablecoins

Some cryptos are pegged to the dollar by design and are always roughly $1. Tether, DAI, or USDC are some examples of this.

These stable coins are a bridge between the crypto and the Fiat world and some people feel more comfortable parking their money here while generating 12% interest.

Chapter 9

Bitcoin Enemies

Bitcoin is a disruptive technology that threatens to replace banks, financial institutions, and Fiat money by doing what they do and more, in a more efficient, faster, and cheaper way.

Obviously, these institutions are not going to just stand there and wait to become obsolete. They'll do anything in their power to fight back and this includes spreading FUD, using political influence, and engaging in dirty play.

Just like the taxi industry doesn't approve of Uber, crony institutions don't approve of bitcoin. Here are some of its biggest enemies

Banks

Banks are the intermediary between the estate and the general public and have a monopoly on money distribution. They live close to political power and to the money machine and this gives them the upper hand.

If you are the only bread maker in town, you don't welcome a new system that allows everyone to make their own bread.

I've often wondered why Apple, Google, or Amazon don't open their own bank or make their own currency. The answer is clear:

regulations. By using political power to build artificial barriers, they try to protect their monopoly and carry on milking the system.

But that was until now.

With bitcoin, you own your money, you don't need permission, and you have access to all the financial services a bank offers and more. Bitcoin is a bank in your pocket.

With crypto and DeFi, you can get up to 12% of interest in deposits and borrow money from 1%. You can transfer money around the world in seconds and almost at no cost, and you can keep your money more secure than the centralized databases of Visa and Mastercard.

Bitcoin is just a better technology and banks are obsolete institutions that are not used to compete. It will be like stealing candy from a kid.

Banks are going the way Blockbuster, Blackberry, and Kodak went, to the dinosaurs' cemetery.

Governments

For some twisted reason, we've let governments all over the world create money when this should have never been their function. Money is whatever the market decides it is. Usually, the most liquid and hardest asset becomes currency, instead of some paper with cultist symbols printed and imposed by the government.

Since Central banks have the power to create money, they don't welcome the debut of hard assets with a sound monetary supply that it's outside their control.

Money is power and they don't want to let it go. The question is: can they do anything about it?

The dollar

Fiat money, but more specifically, the US dollar has enjoyed the supremacy and hegemony of being the world's reserve currency for almost a century. Before that, it was gold and after the dollar, it'll be bitcoin.

The FED and the US government don't like this newcomer and they are trying to stop it with whatever means necessary.

Wall Street

The tycoons of wall street control 90% of large-scale financial operations and they do so in an opaque, elitist, and crony way.

They manipulate the markets at will and make billions in return. When they win, they make a fortune, when they lose, you and I foot the bill.

This was one of the reasons that made Nakamoto create bitcoin - to fight this corrupt and manipulative system of privatizing profits and socializing losses.

Bitcoin allows for trading, speculation, futures, options, and just about any investment transaction that Wall Street does but in a way that is open, transparent, immutable, and permissionless.

No dodgy deals behind closed doors, no preferential treatment, and no insider trading. This is a big threat to the traditional financial industry that is beginning to see huge outflows of money into the crypto world.

The IMF and the World Bank

These two organizations control the flow of credit towards the developing world. In exchange, they extract wealth from these countries and give it to those in charge.

These bureaucratic organizations will cease to exist the moment Fiat money disappears so it's in their best interest to make Bitcoin fail.

When El Salvador announced the decision to adopt bitcoin, the IMF punished them by suspending all credits immediately. This coercive measure can be considered as blackmail and shows how far they are prepared to go to protect their monopoly.

Bitcoin competitors

Bitcoin also has some competitors, there are alternatives that pretend to take away market share from the crypto asset. Some of them are old schools like the dollar or gold, others are more modern like Ethereum or Cardano, and some are very centralized like CDBCs.

Let's look into them one by one.

Gold

Bitcoin shares many characteristics with gold. Both are fungible, scarce, with a high stock to flow ratio, durable, and both represent good stores of value.

But bitcoin is far superior in many ways. It's easier to transfer, transport, secure, verify and subdivide.

In countries where human rights violations are the norm, bitcoin brings freedom and independence to the oppressed while gold just can't. Just by remembering a few words from your seed phrase, no one can take bitcoin away from you. You can cross borders, send it to another country or hide it forever. This would be impossible with any other asset.

However, gold has the upper hand in one scenario - armageddon. If there is no internet and no electricity for prolonged periods then gold would likely conserve its value while bitcoin would probably not.

Apart from the doomsday scenario, bitcoin is a superior asset and it has surpassed gold as a better store of value.

Dollar

The dollar is competing with bitcoin but it's clearly losing. If everything goes as planned, bitcoin will replace the dollar as an international currency. The dollar's only chance of survival is to associate itself with bitcoin and become backed by it as it used to be with gold until 1971.

Altcoins

There have been lots of bitcoin killers over the years, most of them are already dead.

Bitcoin is not easy to kill. There are a number of reasons that make it inexpugnable. The network effect, the first-mover advantage, the true decentralization, the real scarcity, and many more.

Bitcoin is number one as a store of value and will never lose its crown. Altcoins can compete in other niches but not in the main category.

The dollar never felt threatened by the success of startups like Google or Amazon because they compete in different areas. For the same reason, bitcoin is not affected by Cardano, Solana, or ETH because they play in a different league.

These are some of the best bitcoin qualities:

1. It's the best store of value
2. It's truly decentralized
3. It has the biggest Network
4. It has the biggest adoption
5. It benefits from the first-mover advantage

Bitcoin is such a pristine asset that it can only be replaced by better technology. Gold was replaced by the dollar and now both are being replaced by bitcoin. It's unlikely we see something better in our lifetime

Central Bank Digital Currencies (CBDCs)

Central banks and governments are beginning to worry about cryptocurrencies. This is why they have begun to work on their own CBDCs.

CBDCs will succeed, no question about it. They have a captive market after all. Pensions, salaries, taxes, fines, etc will be paid in the official currency and this will give governments total control.

Once they are in place and running, central banks will issue money, put it in your wallet (if you deserve it), and remove any taxes or fines you owe. They'll know exactly where you spend your money and could even deny unauthorized uses.

Let's say you want to buy meat, cigarettes or alcohol which are obviously not good for you. Nanny state will freeze your wallet to protect you from yourself and there is nothing you can do about it.

CBDCs are very scary and act as powerful tools in the hands of the government. I personally will try to opt-out. I read Orwell's novel 1984 in 1984 and was impacted by it. I would rather keep some of my liberties while I can.

As a currency, CBDC will have the same problems as Fiat money, so from a financial point of view, they won't make much sense.

The only way to escape this Orwellian dystopia is to accumulate as much bitcoin as you can before CBDCs are in place. Later, it'll be too late.

CBDCs will render cash and banks unnecessary since there will be a direct link between citizens and central banks, but this will not affect bitcoin. If anything, it'll increase BTC's demand like it does in China. No one wants to live under a surveillance state.

Once CBDCs are here, there will be only two options; compliance with the controlling apparatus or function in a parallel system with bitcoin. Your choice.

Chapter 10

Adoption

Who buys Bitcoin?

The amount of publicly traded companies buying bitcoin keeps growing and they don't just buy a tiny fraction, they buy by the billions. Grayscale (600,000 bitcoins), Microstrategy (100,000 BTC), Tesla (40,000 BTC), Paypal, Square, and even Visa are entering the market.

Recently 300 banks worldwide have announced they will be offering bitcoin funds to their best clients and later on to everyone else. JP Morgan, Goldman & Sachs, Morgan Stanley, and Wells Fargo are some of the biggest banks in the world offering these services.

They hate bitcoin and have spoken evil about it in the past, yet, they can't afford to ignore it any longer. They have been forced to swallow the bitter pill as a desperate attempt to save their businesses.

Also the tech giants - Amazon, Google, and Apple and dipping their toe in. Amazon has been looking for blockchain developers, there are speculations about them releasing their own currency, accepting payments in BTC, and investing in the ecosystem.

Google and Apple already accept payments in crypto and could soon start investing in it. These giants hold huge amounts in cash and not protecting themselves from inflation would be financial suicide.

On top of that, El Salvador is adopting bitcoin as legal tender, Honduras has started installing a network of BTC ATMs, Cuba is about to legalize crypto and move away from the dollar dependency, Paraguay is in talks, and Argentina, Panama, and many others in the region will make a move soon.

Bitcoin is actually the best thing happening to Latin America and could well be the solution to the pervasive inflation problem.

Some people think that bitcoin needs governmental support or at least friendly regulations, but this couldn't be further from the truth. In countries where BTC is not legally welcomed or even partially banned, it is taking off fast. Venezuela, Nigeria, and even China are big adopters of crypto for many reasons, the main one being distrust in their governments and their currency.

Ray Dalio, one of the best investors of all time, recommends having some exposure to BTC in a balanced portfolio and even goes on to say that cash is trash. Warren Buffet who despises anything technological has invested heavily in Fintech companies that are betting on bitcoin.

Everyone is surrendering to it, even those who don't like/understand it. And the surprising thing is that these people are HODLers, they buy as much as they can but they will never sell.

When you hear bitcoin is a scam, a Ponzi scheme, or a bubble, ask yourself: Can the best investors of all time be totally wrong? How likely is this? Am I missing something here?

Is it too late?

There are about 200 million people that own some bitcoin. In addition, there are the investors, companies, and countries mentioned above. But all of them amount to less than 1% of the potential market for crypto, meaning we are still very early.

In a world with 50 million millionaires and 8000 billion people, there is only 21 million bitcoin to go around. There is not even 1 BTC per millionaire and most of them haven't woken up to this fact yet.

Most experts are convinced that bitcoin could easily reach $1 Million by 2030 and from there, shoot to the moon. This is not FOMO or wishful thinking, it's basic math of supply and demand.

Money is migrating from old assets into this new world of crypto and this is going to become the biggest transfer of wealth ever. It's not late at all, this is only just starting.

Game theory

According to game theory, when a player makes a move, the rest are forced to follow suit or risk being left out.

Some countries like El Salvador have already made a move. Some investment funds like Microstrategy have already spent billions. Some individual investors like Ray Dalio are already in.

The rest are now forced to join in, even if they are not ready. Blockbuster didn't understand game theory and they went extinct. Hopefully, some would have learned the lesson by now.

Consequences of bitcoin

Bitcoin is not just a monetary asset or an alternative currency, bitcoin is an ideology that will force politicians to rethink their models and their power structures.

Bitcoin is a quiet revolution that threatens to turn legacy systems upside down and do away with obsolete institutions.

Banks, financial institutions, the FED, Wall Street, the IMF, and the World Bank are top-down institutions based on crony capitalism. So far, we've put up with those because there was no other choice. Until now.

With a system that can replace banks, investment institutions, and governments' Fiat money, the whole thing becomes a new game with new rules. Vertical systems become horizontal, the wealthy will remain rich (if they act quick) but this brings many opportunities for wealth redistribution.

With bitcoin, there are no artificial barriers, dodgy deals behind closed doors, or the favoritism we see in many financial transactions. It's an open, transparent, and free system. Warren Buffett has no other advantage over you than more access to capital, but he will not get any preferential treatment as he does on Wall Street.

Bitcoin is so scarce that just hodling 0.1 BTC will put you in the top 5% of the world's investors. Try that with stocks or gold. Bitcoin is the best asymmetric bet in our lifetime and by taking advantage of it, you will change the world, literally.

Why do the rich invest in bitcoin?

People become wealthy because they have a vision, a strategy and work hard to achieve their goals. You could learn something from them and one day you might be able to retire early and travel the world.

The reason they invest in bitcoin is the same they invest in stocks, real estate, or gold: because they are able to see the potential. If prices are volatile or go down for a while, they don't care because they are here for the long run.

These are some of the rules they follow when investing:

- If you aren't holding it for at least 10 years, don't hold it for 10 mins. Warren Buffet
- When everybody is selling, buy. Most people do the opposite
- Make sure is the right investment, study it deeply, then go full in
- When you get it right, never sell, let it run
- If you can borrow at 3% and invest at 20%, you'll be making a 17% profit (But be careful here)
- Always keep in mind inflation and try to protect yourself from it
- When everyone panics, it's time to buy
- Study trends and disruptive technologies and try to forecast their effects
- Never sell the golden geese

If you think like the poor, you'll always be poor. Try to change your mindset before you go totally broke. Don't let them trick you with the middle-class label. If you are constantly worrying about the future, about scarcity, and about paying your bills, then, you are poor even if you have a high income.

After thinking about this long and hard, I've come to the conclusion that mindset is what makes us wealthy or broke. Take Elon Musk, for example, leave him in the streets of Myanmar with no money, no contacts, and no help, and he'll become wealthy again in less than a year. In fact, that's exactly what he did when he emigrated to the US and was surviving on $1 dollar sandwiches a day.

The main difference between you and him is a mindset. Change your mindset and you'll be unstoppable.

Investors

Wealthy investors find in bitcoin an opportunity to diversify, hedge against inflation, and increase their wealth with the best performing asset ever.

Ray Dalio, Michael Saylor, Elon Musk, Paul Tudor Jones, Raoul Paul, Mike Novogratz, Chamath Palihapitiya, the Winklevoss twins, Barry Silbert, Catie Wood, Robert Kiyosaki, Mark Cuban, and many others are legendary investors leading the way into the crypto world.

They made their fortunes investing in other more traditional assets and now they are moving into bitcoin. Surely, they must see something we are not seeing. Would you bet against them? I wouldn't.

Companies like Microstrategy and Ark Invest are selling their tech stocks in order to buy more bitcoin. There is a shift happening as we speak. Traditional assets are being replaced by the most pristine asset in the 21st century. And yet, most people are oblivious to it.

The trend makers are making a move, the next 5 years will reshape the financial world. This is a lifetime opportunity and we have front-row seats.

Middle class

The poor and the rich understand bitcoin but the middle class finds it harder to grasp.

Those who have become addicted to a monthly salary, 4 weeks of paid leave, a 401k, and a comfortable existence, find it difficult to understand all the fuss about bitcoin.

But that stability, security, and comfort could disappear suddenly. Everything is changing fast, disruptive technologies and exponential growth are dismantling the traditional world. Trying to hold on to the past is a losing battle.

Horse breeders tried to hold on to their industry after the automobile made its debut. They were soon gone.

Crypto is a technology that is here to stay and those who ignore it will be wiped out by the bitcoin tsunami. Learn to surf before it's too late.

How much is enough?

People often ask me how much bitcoin should they buy. The conservative answer is: as much as they can afford to lose.

Like any investment, we should always fathom the possibility of total loss even though if the chances of it happening are very slim.

As a hedge against inflation or a recession, the usual advice is to put 10-20% of your liquid network into bitcoin. More adventurous investors increase their stake even higher the more they understand the technology. Some investors like Raoul Paul have admitted to being "irresponsibly bullish" on crypto.

Here are some figures for reference (at today's prices):

- Owning 0.037 BTC ($1,500) will put you above the average
- 0.135 BTC ($5,040) will put you in the top 5%
- 3.63 BTC ($150,000) will put you in the top 1%

I personally think that everyone that can afford it should buy at least half a bitcoin and hodl it for at least 10 years. Doing that will probably be the best investment decision ever.

Chapter 11

How to get Bitcoin

There are several ways to acquire bitcoin. The most common is to buy it at an exchange but there are also other methods.

Mining bitcoin

This is not recommended for beginners. Back in the day, it was possible to mine bitcoin with an old laptop and get 50 coins a day. Unfortunately, those days are gone.

Now, mining is an expensive operation that is done in specialized farms with hundreds of computer equipment (Asics) that compete with each other to solve mathematical puzzles in order to obtain BTC as a reward.

These mining farms are usually colocated near power stations, hydroelectric dams, solar or wind farms. Basically, near abundant power sources supply electricity at a low cost.

Is it still profitable to mine at home?

For bitcoin probably not, unless you have access to a very cheap energy source or you join a mining aggregator where the resources from thousands of miners get combined into a pool.

For other coins, like Ethereum Classic, Litecoin, or Raven Coin, there is less competition and it can still be profitable. It's just a matter of studying the market, price, electricity cost, and working out some numbers. But unless you are technically inclined I would advise against it.

Earning Bitcoin

One way to acquire bitcoin is by getting paid in it. Whatever you do for a living, you could negotiate with your customers or boss to be paid in crypto. This is actually easier than it sounds and it can bring benefits to both parties.

For example, if you are doing some work online and your customer is in another country, instead of going through the hassle of wiring money, exchange rates, and commissions, the money could be sent directly to your wallet instantly and at almost no cost.

Bitcoin is gaining in popularity for international transfers since banks and Fiat money are not really suited for this.

Buying bitcoin

Obviously, the easiest and most direct way of acquiring bitcoin is by buying it at an **exchange**. Kraken, Coinbase, Binance, and FTX are some of the best-known platforms and the transactions are fairly straightforward.

Perhaps, the hardest part of buying crypto is opening an account. Most countries demand the Know Your Customer procedure (KYC) where you have to facilitate personal and financial data, upload a few photos and documents, etc.

Once that's done, it's just a matter of sending money from your bank account or credit card and then buying some coins of your fancy.

All of the aforementioned are proper crypto exchanges. They offer investment options as well as custody of your coins. Also, if you wish, you can transfer your crypto out of the exchange and into a cold wallet where you control your own keys.

In general, it's advisable to withdraw your coins from exchanges and put them into a cold wallet like Trezor or Ledger. A cold wallet is the most secure way to keep your crypto providing you take the necessary precautions.

Alternatively, there are other places where you can acquire some crypto. Fintech and trading companies like Revolut, CashApp, Paypal, or eToro offer these services although they are not proper crypto exchanges. These companies don't offer a wallet and the coins are kept in a common pool. In order to withdraw your money, you have to convert it to Fiat first.

Nothing wrong with that if you just want to buy and sell small amounts and are a short-term investor. But ideally, being able to withdraw your crypto is an important feature.

I use Revolut and sometimes I buy small amounts of crypto there, but most of my assets come from proper exchanges. In the future, Revolut and all the other fintech companies out there will offer a wallet, but until then, I'll keep using the crypto exchanges.

One thing to keep in mind for beginners is that you don't have to buy a whole bitcoin. You can buy anything from 0.0002 BTC ($10) and keep accumulating over time. In fact, this is actually the best investment strategy in the long run and it's called DCA.

This ecosystem is fastly moving and by the time this book is published some of the details will be obsolete. To see the latest news, you can check my blog: albertoguerrero.net where I write specific articles about some aspects of crypto.

HODLing

HODL in the Bitcoin lingo is the term to refer to the act of buying bitcoin and holding it forever.

This might sound counterintuitive but when you understand the market, it makes a lot of sense.

We are emotional animals and get played by fear and greed. This is the reason most people lose money when investing in liquid markets like securities - they buy high (Greed) and then sell low (Fear).

But once you study an asset like bitcoin and understand the fundamentals, you realize that it doesn't matter so much at what price you bought, what matters is how long you hold it.

With bitcoin, no one who bought and hodl for at least 4 years lost any money, in fact, most made a small fortune.

When you buy a pristine asset that is so scarce, you should never get rid of it. It'd be like owning real estate in manhattan. Why would you sell when it keeps appreciating forever?

Besides, when you sell bitcoin, you are buying Fiat. Selling something that appreciates 200% annually to buying something that devalues 20% a year, makes no sense. It'd be like selling gold to buy manure.

The big question here is: If I never sell, what's the point of investing?

I hear you, I asked myself exactly the same question a long time ago, and here's the answer: **do as the rich do.** When wealthy investors find the right asset, they never sell it, they borrow against it and use it as collateral.

This way, not only do you get to keep the asset and benefit from future appreciation, but also you pay no tax since borrowing is not a taxable event.

There are crypto platforms like Celsius or BlockFi that allow you to borrow money from 1% interest when using crypto as collateral.

This is an advanced concept and not easy to grasp by the average Joe, but just keep in mind that the possibility exists and you can take advantage of it once your coins are a big part of your portfolio.

In the Youtube channel Invest Answers there is a video called "How to retire on crypto" where James works out some interesting numbers. Have a look and see what you think.

Taxes

One of the reasons the middle and working class will never be wealthy is taxes. Proportionally, employees pay the highest tax rates. In addition, there is very little leeway to reduce this burden.

The rich on the other hand, put strategies in place to minimize taxes legally and often end up paying nothing.

One of the important differences here is that employees pay income tax while companies only pay tax on capital gains. You can't avoid having a salary (unless you fire yourself) but it's easy to avoid capital gains.

Events like selling a house or stocks for a profit are taxable events but others like borrowing against assets are not.

If you don't have an income and never sell your assets, you can legally save a fortune in taxes over a lifetime.

This is one of the reasons people buy and HODL bitcoin. No taxable event and means no tax. When you need liquidity, just borrow against the asset and use it as collateral. If the market continues as expected, you could live off your bitcoin forever.

Where to Keep Your Bitcoin

There are several ways to HODL your bitcoin, here are the most common.

Exchanges

Exchanges like Kraken, Coinbase, or Binance are fairly secure custodians providing you follow the security protocol properly - two-factor authentication, secure passwords, phone & email confirmation, and vault protection.

Having said that, you should not leave a lot of money in exchanges since they are centralized and online and therefore susceptible to attacks.

Cold wallet

Cold wallets are by far the most secure way to store your crypto. Being offline ensures no hacker can have access to your money and this eliminates 99.9% of threats.

To access your funds, you need a 6 digit code for the standard wallet and on top of that, you can also have a hidden wallet inside the cold wallet that nobody knows about, adding an extra layer of security.

In case your wallet gets lost or damaged, you can recover your funds by using another device and a 24-word seed phrase. In fact, this is what makes your assets bulletproof. Just by remembering this seed phrase, you can recover your funds anywhere in the world as long as you have internet access.

Now, with power, comes responsibility. If you forget or lose your seed phrase or your password and somebody gets access to it, your funds could be lost forever.

With a cold wallet, you are the weakest link. But provided you follow some basic rules, your money will be safe. The coins in your wallet are in fact safer than all the gold stored in Fort Knox.

For people living under oppressive regimes, bitcoin is freedom. Just by knowing a few words, they can escape tyranny and leave the country with all their assets intact.

How to borrow against bitcoin

Platforms like Celsius or BlockFi allow the possibility of borrowing against your crypto and get some liquidity. Money can be borrowed from 1% interest providing you have enough collateral. This is a great way to get some cash without having to sell your assets.

However, when you borrow using collateral, you are taking some risks. Let's see some examples.

You have $1000 in Ethereum and want to borrow $200 (20% collateral). If the price of ETH goes below $200 (an 80% drop) you get liquidated and lose the lot. However, this is an unlikely scenario because volatility tends to decrease as the asset matures. Nevertheless, this is something to keep in mind. Besides, you could avoid liquidation by adding more funds to your account when you get the margin call.

But if you take a 50% margin, i.e. borrowing $500 against your $1000 funds, then the risk is much higher. A 50% drop does happen from time to time so this is not advisable. Generally speaking, you should never borrow more than 20% of your capital unless you have other funds that you can use to avoid liquidation.

Interest

Another way to provide an income with crypto is by lending it to others. These same platforms, Celsius and BlockFi, provide this service and can pay interest up to 12 % on stable coins and 5-6% on crypto.

However, unlike borrowing, lending produces a profit and it's therefore taxable. Keep this in mind.

Staking

And the third option to get some yield is to stake your crypto. Staking is basically lending your coins in order to help secure the network. For example, in Kraken, staking Polkadot or Kusama offer rewards of 12% APY. This is another option to consider in order to get some passive income.

How to Invest in Bitcoin

The best strategy for investing is probably DCA (Dollar Cost Averaging). This consists of buying a fixed small amount of crypto every month regardless of the price.

Let's say that you can spare $100 dollar every month. On the first day of every month, you use those dollars to buy your favorite coin. By doing it this way, you avoid emotional trading - fear and greed - and on average it produces remarkably good results.

For example, had you been investing $100 a month in BTC since 2010, you'd have spent $13,600 and your capital would be now $13.7 billion, with an ROI of 101,000,000%. Not bad at all.

Don't get obsessed with the price, buy little and often. Eventually, it will pay off and you'll be able to sleep at night.

Is it worth investing in Bitcoin?

If you are reading this book it is because you are at least considering investing, wondering if this is for you, and pondering the risks vs the rewards.

Like any other investment, bitcoin is risky but not investing in bitcoin, is even riskier.

When you don't own bitcoin, you are investing in Fiat, a currency that is being devalued as we speak. Your dollars in the bank are losing 15% annually and this trend will continue for the next 10 years.

This is risky.

The alternatives

Gold has been stagnant for a long time. Now with the competition from bitcoin, it will struggle even more.

The stock market is in a bubble created by money printing. It might or might not burst, but the risk is quite high. If it takes a dive, it could be a good opportunity to enter and buy the dip but until then, best to stay away.

Real estate is usually a good investment providing you choose the right location and you wait long enough. The possibility of financing makes property an interesting option for those with no access to capital.

On the negative side, houses are a nightmare of taxes, maintenance, and hidden costs. Besides, you run the risk of location, what happens if the city/neighborhood/country becomes unfashionable?

Property is a young person's game. When you are 30, it makes sense to buy a house, when you are 50 not so much.

Looking at the alternatives, we can see that not only bitcoin is the best investment, but also the rest are not very exciting at all.

There is no other asset with the potential, the future, and the technology of bitcoin.

Bitcoin is speculative but with solid fundamentals behind it.

Bitcoin is risky but with lots of potentials.

Bitcoin is more liquid, more profitable, and less risky than any other asset out there. You should consider placing at least 10% of your money in bitcoin.

In the 90s, we saw internet companies like Google and Amazon taking off. It seemed risky and most people didn't dare to invest. Now, we have a second chance with bitcoin, only this time it will go higher and faster. The internet adoption curve is very similar to the current bitcoin adoption curve. In 1998, only 1% of the public was using the internet, exactly where bitcoin is right now. This means that BTC could get to 60% adoption in just a few years.

So far, only 200 million people have invested in bitcoin, and every week, 3 more million join in. We are now at the beginning of the curve, just about when it's starting to become exponential.

Bitcoin is not just an investment, it's a technology that will transform the world, that will replace obsolete industries, and that will bring hope for those in need.

Bitcoin is the best asymmetric bet in the history of humankind. It's the pinnacle of human invention. Satoshi Nakamoto should've won the Nobel prize for economics, IT, and cryptography.

Forget about the price, bitcoin is a great asset even if it doesn't appreciate at all. It provides a solution to many of the problems humans have been dealing with since the dawn of time. Finally, we can transfer money peer to peer without the need for intermediaries, in a permissionless, trustless, and secure way. This is the most revolutionary financial technology ever invented and not taking part in this revolution would be a huge mistake.

Chapter 12

Who should NOT buy Bitcoin?

Bitcoin is not for everybody. If you identify yourself with any of the following characteristics then you are probably not ready yet.

Speculation

If you think Bitcoin is a fast way to riches, then you should not invest. Bitcoin could make you rich but it will take time and effort. You should be prepared for HODLing for at least 10 years. If you are in a hurry, buy a lottery ticket and good luck.

Fear

If you are fearful and panic when your investment goes down, then you should not buy bitcoin. This asset is still volatile and will continue to go up and down for a while.

Learn how it works and then your fear will be mitigated by knowledge. It doesn't seem like a rollercoaster when you understand the fundamentals.

Naivety

If you believe what the government, the news, the bankers, and the think tanks tell you to believe, then you are too naive. Keep your money in the bank, earn a generous 0.1%, ignore inflation, and hope for the best.

Bitcoin is for rebels, for nonconformists, for the brave, and for those who think differently. If you don't question everything from the status quo, from society, and from the way you live your life then, bitcoin is not for you. Carry on being obedient and hopefully, the nanny estate will take care of you.

No money

If you have no money at all, then you just can't invest. But you have to ask yourself, why did you let yourself get into this situation? And how can you get out of it?

Nowadays, if you speak English and have access to the internet, you could be making money online if you dare to put yourself out there. Start a Youtube channel, share what you know, write, podcast, learn, become a side hustler. Use that extra income to improve your life and with the rest, invest for the future.

Everybody should have some savings for a rainy day and even put away 10% of their income every month. If you don't, you need to work on that first.

However tempting it is, do not use leverage to invest. Do not bet with money you don't have in the hope of big earnings. That's the wrong way to do it.

Leverage is borrowing money you don't have. It's possible to use it in the stock market, in crypto, and even in real estate. For example, let's say you want to buy bitcoin but you only have $100. You could use 10x leverage and buy $1000 worth of BTC. If it goes up great, but if it goes just 10% down you lose the lot.

Just don't be greedy. Be patient and make a plan.

Comfort

If you like to stay in your comfort zone, remain within familiar territory, and avoid challenges, then bitcoin is not your thing.

Bitcoin is a revolution, it's going to change everything we take for granted. All systems that you use now - banks, investments, Fiat money - will be transformed beyond recognition.

However, this is happening with or without you, so might as well join in or at least stay informed.

Comfort is the biggest dream killer. Get out of your comfort zone or you'll miss out on life.

Centralization

If you like centralized organizations like the European Union, the Federal Reserve, or the IMF and their top-down policies, then bitcoin is not for you.

Bitcoin is the most decentralized system made by humans. There is no one in charge and it can't be attacked since there is nothing to attack. It's a very robust network that provides a lot of resilience and freedom but you have to do your bit. You can't call customer service to complain if you lose your coins. Get educated and accept responsibility or stay with your bank and fill in that application form for a new loan.

Charity

If you think that Unicef, the Red Cross, or the world bank are doing a great job fighting poverty, then you still don't get it.

Bitcoin provides the fishing rod, not the fish. Giving people the tools to escape poverty instead of handouts is what works.

Until the developing world stops using broken money, nothing we or they do will amount to anything. First, fix the money problem, then the rest will follow.

Bitcoin is not for the fearful, the cautious, the weak, or the obedient.

Bitcoin is for the rebels, the brave, the nonconformists, and the visionary.

If you are not one of those, re-educate yourself and then you'll be ready to enter this world. If not, you'll have to keep tasting the bitter pill of mediocrity.

We've all been there. We've been educated to be obedient, fearful, and sheepish but it's your responsibility to escape that trap and release your full potential.

Up to you.

The Social Side of Bitcoin

Bitcoin is Freedom

Unfortunately, there are still too many authoritarian regimes all over the world that engage in oppressive practices against their citizens.

One of the most effective ways to achieve this oppression is by controlling the money supply. Devaluation, confiscation, inflation, and money printing are some of the tools they use to remain in power.

Without money, there is no power. These oppressed citizens can't even manage to organize themselves to fight back or even consider leaving the country when they don't have any hard assets.

The right to property is a fundamental human right, without it, we have nothing.

Holding Bolivars or any other worthless money means nothing because they have no value. It doesn't matter how hard people work if they get paid in a hyperinflationary currency.

They'll never be able to save money, invest in a small business, educate their children or have any hopes to escape poverty.

The Argentinian peso has been devalued 20 times in recent history. Venezuela has 2,500% inflation. What future can they expect unless they escape the money trap?

Bitcoin fixes this.

Now, in Nigeria, Vietnam, Venezuela, and many other places people have started to stack Sats. They understand how valuable a proper currency is and how it helps to hope for a better future.

No money, no freedom

80% of the world's currencies are a joke. They are not worth the paper they've been printed on. This is why the unbanked get the value of bitcoin instantly and they are leading the world in adoption.

But governments don't like a currency they can't control, so in some cases, they try to ban it or stop it. But they can't. They are powerless against a currency that is totally decentralized, peer to peer and encrypted. The fact that no central authority is involved in the process makes it very resilient.

Even China has tried to ban bitcoin many times with limited success. The fact they keep trying shows that the ban is not really working. They banned Google once and that was it, but bitcoin is banned every other month, proving is censorship-resistant.

Bitcoin is the biggest wealth redistribution opportunity in financial history.

Bitcoin is green

Despite the narrative from the media about bitcoin consuming too much electricity, the fact remains that it is greener than any of the alternatives is poised to replace.

Bitcoin is a big consumer of renewable energy and together there is a lot of symbioses. The problem with solar, wind, and hydro is intermittency. They only produce when the sun is shining, the wind blowing, or the river flowing.

Batteries are still too expensive to be feasible. Bitcoin draws the excess energy, converts it into monetary energy, and this way nothing gets wasted.

All over the world, there are sources of stranded energy that can't find any use and now all that it's been consumed by the miners. It's a win-win situation.

Also because mining is a profitable business, they often promote the construction of renewable projects which then, are used to mine bitcoin and supply the local grid. El Salvador has just recently started mining using geothermal energy from volcanoes. They are creating wealth from clean energy and this is just one of many examples.

Bitcoin aims to replace the banking industry, traditional financial services, gold, and even Fiat money. These industries are far more polluting than a few servers running some code. The more market-share bitcoin gains, the greener the planet will become.

Everything digital is always cleaner than the physical equivalent. Electronic money is better than paper money, Netflix is better than DVDs, ebooks are better than books, remote working is better than working in an office and the list goes on. The world is going digital and that's great news for the planet.

Weak currencies

President Bukele of El Salvador became a hero for the bitcoin community the day he announced the adoption of bitcoin as legal tender in his country.

This is a historical event. Never before has a non-Fiat currency been regarded with legal status. Many have seen this as the beginning of the end for Fiat.

Now it's spreading everywhere, Panama, Ucrania, Nigeria, Zimbabwe, Argentina and many more are eager to make similar moves. Pandora's box has been opened and now there is no return.

What advantages does it bring for these countries?

- Inflation. With bitcoin, prices go down, not up. In Venezuela, you need a sack full of notes to buy bread, with bitcoin only a few Satoshis
- Corruption. Due to the transparency and immutability of the blockchain, dodgy deals behind closed doors become very difficult and this will probably reduce corruption
- Remittances. $1 Trillion is sent every year to help relatives in developing countries. Of that, 25% get lost in commissions to Western Union and the like. With bitcoin, transfers take seconds and cost is almost zero
- Tourism. Currency exchange is a hassle and a scam. Many people would be more inclined to visit places where bitcoin is accepted as payment. El Salvador tourism industry is booming now thanks to bitcoin
- Economy. No country can be taken seriously when they use a broken currency. With bitcoin, the international image projected will improve, and with it GDP, trade, investments, and so on

Bitcoin could well be the trigger that makes all these developing countries improve their situation and grow their finances. Without a strong currency, no economy can do well, but with bitcoin things could improve a lot.

I'm bullish in Latinoamerica after decades of stagnation. I reckon this is what they need to have a fighting chance

Chapter 13

How to Participate in the Ecosystem

There are many ways to benefit from this new technology. The most obvious is buy and HODL but there are many more. Let's see some of them.

Development

If you know how to code or you think you can learn, there are plenty of opportunities to participate in the crypto ecosystem.

Bitcoin is programmable money and Ethereum and others even more so. The possibilities are endless, from smart contracts to applications in the lighting network, new tokens, NFTs, Dapps, Daos, etc. This is like the internet in the 90s, everything needs doing. The infrastructure is just starting to develop and thousands of engineers will be needed.

If you can program the blockchain, you'll never be out of work and the salaries are amazing.

Even if you are not a coder, consider spending a few months learning the ropes so you can get your foot in the door. Once you start with an entry-level job, you are in and the future is going to be bright.

Promotion

There is also high demand for people that can explain this new technology to the masses and promote projects and applications in different industries.

Entrepreneurs, consultants, marketers, and many other professions are needed to initiate and develop new projects. Anybody with a keen interest in the crypto world can participate and make a good income from it. The possibilities are endless.

For example, in El Salvador, every business accepts payments in bitcoin. It has taken a huge effort to educate, promote and train people and businesses to use this new ecosystem. Now it's happening in many other places and they need you to make it happen.

DeFi

Everything considered traditional finance - trading, investing, loans, futures, options, etc - is moving to the crypto world and eventually to decentralized finance (DeFi).

Decentralized platforms are more secure, cheaper, faster, and more efficient but most importantly, they can't be manipulated like Wall Street.

It's still early days and teething problems are to be expected but, like any new sound technology, DeFi will take over and change the world.

Most of the crypto transactions now are being done in Centralized Exchanges like Kraken, Binance, or Coinbase, but soon enough the market will move from CeFi to DeFi so there is plenty of opportunity in this area.

Smart Contracts

Smart contracts are legal agreements that get activated when certain conditions are met. In a way, they are equivalent to traditional contracts but the former can be automated and work unsupervised once they have been activated.

Smart contracts are written in the blockchain and are therefore immutable, programmable and transparent.

There is a lot of work to be done and lawyers and business people will have a lot to contribute to this ecosystem.

The Blockchain

One day, everything will be in the blockchain. From your birth certificate to your house deeds, to food traceability, to electronic voting.

Anything written here is transparent, public, and immutable. Identity theft, for example, will become a thing of the past. There are many applications that now rely on an obsolete centralized system that will migrate to the blockchain.

Again, this transfer will need thousands of people helping out to achieve a successful migration. The opportunities in the blockchain are endless.

How to explain Bitcoin to a friend

If you've read this far, it's because you have some interest and curiosity about participating in this new ecosystem. Whether it's investing, learning, working, or promoting it, you will have to explain to others what you do and why you do it.

When you are convinced about the benefits of this technology, you will want to share your knowledge and help others benefit from this fantastic opportunity.

That's exactly what I'm doing right now. Becoming rich and successful on your own is no fun. We need to spread the word, let others know how to escape the rat race and reclaim freedom.

If we don't, we'll be accused of being selfish, elitist, and greedy. Besides, bitcoin is really good for the disadvantaged, for the planet, and for wealth redistribution. Not defending bitcoin is morally wrong.

You can start explaining the opportunities and possibilities as an investment, as a technology, and as a way of life.

Money is a fundamental part of everyone's life and, why not use a much better version than the old corrupt Fiat currencies?

You can start by recommending this book (if you like it). You can lend it to others or tell them to contact me. I will send them this book for free if they can't afford it. I didn't write this book to make money, I wrote it to share what I know. I believe in the moral case for bitcoin and that's why I evangelize about it.

But before they read this or any other book out there, you will have to introduce some basic concepts about bitcoin to see if this entices their appetite.

These are some of the arguments and counterarguments I use to explain the benefits of Bitcoin.

It's not a bubble

Despite what you hear in the news, bitcoin is not a bubble, a Ponzi scheme, a pyramid, or a scam.

Bitcoin has been around 12 years and that is a long time. Technology breakthroughs sink or swim very quickly and this has been swimming very fast for over a decade.

In these 12 years, it has gone from 0 to $64,000, it has gained more than 200 million users, it has developed a network with thousands of nodes and it's been adopted by public traded companies, banks, millionaires, and sovereign states.

It's not a bubble because the demand keeps growing exponentially while the supply remains limited. It's not a Ponzi because it's decentralized. It's not pure speculation because it has many important use cases the market demands. And is not a scam because nobody is in charge.

Ray Dalio, Michael Saylor, and Cathie Wood have invested billions in this currency and they are among the wealthiest and the best investors of all time. Do you think they would invest in a bubble?

Don't listen to the naysayers. These people invested in the internet, in Apple, in Google, and in Amazon. None of those were bubbles. Now, they have discovered the next big thing and are betting all their money on it. Also, they have declared their intention to HODL forever.

Scarcity

There are only 21 million BTC in total, of which 18.8 are already in circulation. 4 to 7 million have been lost, and most people buy and HODL in cold storage. This leaves us with just 2 million coins available in the exchanges and 8 billion people wanting to buy. With such limited supply and the increasing demand, the price is set to explode in the next few years.

Then, you have the big whales that buy by the billions. Grayscale owns 600,000 BTC and Microstrategy 100,000 BTC.

Soon it will be very difficult to get 1 whole coin, it's estimated that only 300,000 people could ever become whole-coiners.

Even investment funds, pension funds, and institutional investors are beginning to warm up to the idea. Banks like JP Morgan o Goldman&Sachs are recommending their best customers to invest in crypto.

Right now, the total market cap is almost $1 Trillion but in the future, it could go to $100 Trillion. The price could easily get to $100,000 by the end of this cycle (mid-2022) and to $1 Million by 2030.

Knowing this potential and the high probability of it happening makes it almost compulsory to participate. Even taking into account the risk, it's irresponsible not to invest.

Bitcoin is the biggest redistribution of wealth in the history of mankind. Are you going to miss it?

The poor

If you care about the third world, the children starving in Africa, and the death toll from preventable diseases, then you should support bitcoin.

One of the biggest problems in the developing world is a broken financial system, corrupt officials, and inflationary currencies. Bitcoin fixes all this in one go.

These people already know how promising bitcoin is and are betting on it big time. The majority of peer-to-peer transactions are done in developing nations by people that understand that a currency that can't be devalued, confiscated, or censored is a great asset to hold.

Bitcoin solves the problem of the bankless, allowing them access to financial services from which they were banned before. They can buy, sell, invest, borrow and lend small amounts in order to trade, finance their business or buy food.

And let's not forget the remittances market. Western Union is losing $400 million a year in commissions just in El Salvador because now people are using the Lighting network to transfer money around. Those $400 million will go to the families in need. This is a big deal.

I'm very bullish on Latin America, Africa, and Asia. Once they get rid of their weak currencies and embrace bitcoin, the geopolitical map can be turned on its head. I for one would be supporting this cause.

I would like to see that children don't go to bed hungry thanks to bitcoin. Wouldn't you?

Capítulo 14

Wallets

Once we have bought some bitcoin it is time to ensure we don't lose it.

The best way to do this is by using a cold wallet. The exchanges I mention here are very safe, however, nothing is 100% hackerproof. *Not your keys, not your coins* is the motto in the bitcoin community.

There are two types of wallets, hot and cold. Hot wallets are more convenient and easier to use but cold wallets offer an extra layer of security.

Let's see the different possibilities.

Cold Wallets

There are a number of companies producing cold wallets but the ones I can recommend are Trezor and Ledger. They have a good safety record and have been around for long enough to make a reputation.

Of the two, Trezor is open source and for me, that's important because there are more eyes overseeing the project. On the other hand, Ledger supports a wider number of coins so if you are into Altcoins, this is probably a better choice.

They both cost around $60 in their basic model and both come with detailed instructions on how to set up and implement security strategies.

Remember, with this, you are 100% in control of your money but with freedom comes responsibility. If you lose your keys and your wallet, you lose your money.

But don't be intimidated by this, just follow the instructions and your coins will be safe.

Multisig

One extra layer of security can be provided by a system called Multisig. By having several cold wallets spread in different geographical locations and setting up a multi-signature system, your crypto will be even more secure.

Typically, in a multisig arrangement, you will have let's say 5 wallets and in order to move your funds, you'll need a majority vote or 3 wallets. If you keep one wallet, give another wallet to someone you trust, and leave the third with a custody service then, even if the other two wallets go missing or stolen, no one would be able to withdraw the funds.

It sounds complicated but it's not. Once you have a certain amount of crypto it's recommended you use these services.

Hot wallet

Another alternative is to store your keys in the cloud in a hot wallet like Electrum or Mycelium. There is always the risk of the system being hacked but generally speaking these companies are well protected.

The advantage of using these services is that there is more backup in case you lose your keys and being online it's just more convenient. At the end of the day, there is a trade-off between security and convenience and that's a decision you have to make.

Chapter 15

Financial Education

The rich and the poor understand bitcoin quickly, it's the middle class that offers more resistance. If you live in the developed world, have 3 bank accounts, 5 credit cards, and have access to all financial services, it will take you longer to see the advantages of cryptocurrencies.

However, if you live in a country with hyperinflation, confiscation, and censorship, you get this rather quickly.

The rich are used to investing so they understand the benefits of a scarce asset with growing demand.

But sometimes, middle-class privileged citizens could do with a reality check. I strongly believe that most of us are financially illiterate but our comfortable lives don't prompt us to seek this most needed education.

You were told to go to school, get a good degree, a well-paid job, save, get a mortgage and invest for retirement. Nothing wrong with that, but if you follow that path you will never be free.

A job for life is a thing of the past, your house is not an asset but a liability, your pension is broken and the money you have in the bank is losing purchasing power as we speak.

The American dream is a fantasy used to sell you financial products. Now, you have become a slave and there is no way out. Wake up because things are about to turn ugly.

The middle class is trapped in their lives by one strong emotion: Fear.

Fear is what keeps you going to work every morning to a job you hate, it's what makes you keep contributing to your pension despite knowing that you are throwing money away. It's what makes you keep paying your mortgage despite knowing you will never recover the capital invested.

Fear is a bad advisor. You have the ability and the potential to do better in life but you will never do it unless you face your insecurities.

Nobody is going to save your ass this time, you are on your own. Not the government, not your company, and not God. You either devise a plan B or you and your family could be in deep trouble.

But for that, you need to understand how the world works and how it differs from what you've been told.

The only way out of this mess is to develop an entrepreneurial mindset, learn to understand risk and be willing to take action.

Luckily, you have access to the internet, and with it a world full of possibilities. Nowadays you can learn anything for free and start taking advantage of the opportunities around you.

Technology and crypto are just some of the options but there are many more. Anyone with a willingness to learn can start making money on the side in months. YouTube, blogging, teaching, courses, freelancing, etc. The sky's the limit.

When people hear this, they often shy away and discard this as risky, too much hassle, too late, or too difficult. These are just excuses. Deep down is all down to fear.

You know that you can do a lot more than you are currently doing. You know you are leaving a lot of potential on the proverbial table. You know that the clock is ticking and eventually you will have to face your fears.

Would you rather be in charge of your destiny rather than have to rely on the decisions of strangers?

The world is becoming very unpredictable. AI, automation, crypto, and many other technologies threaten to disrupt your way of life. Being prepared for what is coming is not only useful but compulsory.

When you are left stranded with no job, no pension, and no house, how are you going to react?

Burying your head in the sand won't cut it this time. You know well what is coming and you should get ready for it. This time you are on your own.

If you understand technology, social media, digital marketing and develop an entrepreneurial spirit, you'll do fine no matter what life throws at you. If you don't...what are you waiting for? Start learning today.

First, you will have to get rid of the old scripts like: "money is not important", "better the devil you know" and "the tall poppy gets cut".

These are just old-fashioned scripts made in the industrial era that serve no purpose nowadays. Now, you have to put yourself out there, get noticed, make your voice heard and claim your piece of the pie.

The sheep mentality is dead, now you need to be a wolf.

Often when I speak to my friends I hear replies like "It is what it is" "What can we do?" and other such defeatist pearls.

It is what YOU want it to be. And YOU can do a lot to change your circumstances.

But change requires effort, new habits have to be developed and old habits discarded. Your ego will offer plenty of resistance to keep you cozy in your bubble but you must fight back.

The world as we know it is imploding. The government, the economy, college, the job market, the financial industry are not what they used to be. Everything is being undermined by technology.

The future is here whether you like it or not. Reinvent yourself or you'll have a hard time surviving.

In order to survive this societal collapse, we must create parallel universes where the conventional rules don't apply. Crypto is one of them but not the only one.

The Fiat system, the banking industry, and financial services are going through a deep crisis and might not survive. Putting all your eggs in the Fiat basket is financial suicide.

Bitcoin will replace most currencies, most financial services, and maybe even gold. The blockchain will become ubiquitous, soon anything that holds some value will be stored in the public ledger.

This is a profound transformation that forces us to adapt and change our mindsets. Now, understating your own psychology and why you behave the way you do is paramount.

This is scary I know. But from chaos comes opportunity. Everything needs to be done in order to migrate to the crypto universe and you could be one of the pioneers.

Stop wasting your time with mindless entertainment and start taking action. Learn, experiment, focus, research, share, but above all open your mind and start from a blank slate.

How to retrain yourself

Start reading about the economy, finances, entrepreneurship, psychology, and technology. Learn to think for yourself, don't be a sheep. Question everything. Take nothing as dogma.

I have learned a lot from Kiyosaki, Tim Ferris, Altucher, Ray Dalio, Taleb, Harari, and many others.

But you don't have to follow these people, find your own tribe. The important thing is that you expose yourself to timeless wisdom that offers a different perspective from the standard education.

What was good for the 19th century, won't cut it in the 21st century.

But I would argue that the main barrier to success and happiness is that voice in your head that keeps telling you that you are not good enough, that you are an impostor, and that you can't afford to dream.

That's Bullshit.

We've been brainwashed to believe that all we can do is play by the rules and accept our mediocre destiny, to be a soldier and take commands, and to never question authority or the status quo.

How convenient is that? Of course, those in power would want you to believe such garbage. A grateful slave is always more useful.

But it's your responsibility to wake up from your slumber and start designing your life the way it was meant to be and not the way they designed it for you.

There are many ways to gain this freedom and independence but bitcoin is one of the best.

Despite what you might have been led to believe, money is important and the kind of money that can't be manipulated by the central banks is even more important.

If you decide to become an entrepreneur (and you should), charging for your services in bitcoin will be a great start.

Bitcoin makes you free. It offers financial independence, an alternative system, growth potential, disruptive technology, and a safe haven against an inefficient and obsolete system.

If bitcoin is for you, make sure you take action and participate in some of the opportunities and avenues the ecosystem provides.

Financial independence

You are poor. You might disagree but if you have to get up every morning to do a job you hate, if you penny-pinch through life in order to have a nest egg, if you daydream about a 2-week vacation in the Caribbean then, you are not free, you are not independent, and you are in the 99% basket.

If you are an employee, you are at the mercy of others' decisions and your financial stability is hanging from a thread.

In the current economic climate, it is very risky to depend on one source of income. You must try and find some side hustles that give you enough leverage to quit one day and move to greener pastures.

It's also important that these side hustles are your own business. You don't want to have more bosses, you want to be your own boss.

Having your own blog, youtube channel, or podcast are excellent options that provide scalability, creative freedom, and the opportunity to reach out to millions and make your voice heard.

A job can pay $50/hour, a youtube channel with 100,000 followers could potentially provide you with a scalable source of income for years to come.

Your local butcher works as hard as Elon Musk but the latter do scalable things while the former doesn't. Always pursue enterprises with exponential possibilities.

Bitcoin is leverage

Give me a lever and I'll move the world.

Arquimedes

Bitcoin is that leverage. With it, you'll be able to rock your world and achieve your goals not just as an investment but also as an opportunity to work, research, learn and develop new projects.

Options like DeFi, NFTs, automated investments, smart contracts, creating your own token, and many more. The sky's the limit, the possibilities are endless. This is literally like the internet in the 90s.

If you have money, invest it in bitcoin. If you don't, participate in the ecosystem and create value. You will not find another opportunity like this in your lifetime.

Contrarian

We've been brought up to become obedient, useful, and standard, but this education won't serve you very well in the 21st century.

You have to develop your own views about reality and this often means going against the grain.

Becoming a contrarian is necessary for survival in a world full of lemmings. Don't be a cog in the machine, be a creator, an inventor, and an artist.

Elon Musk, Einstein, Steve Jobs, Christopher Columbus, Galileo, Leonardo DaVinci, Jesus Christ, Gandhi, and many more were contrarians. They had a vision about the world, they didn't like the status quo, they fought against the system and that's why we remember them.

But you don't have to be a genius to leave your mark, you just have to know what you want and keep at it whatever it takes.

For example, most people would agree that the current financial system is broken, and yet, they keep counting their pennies and hoping for the best. That's not the way to do it. Now with bitcoin, there is an opportunity to leave the sinking boat and swim to the island of freedom. There you can start your life from scratch.

Bitcoin promises to redistribute wealth and power and give a chance to those that got the short straw in life. Bitcoin is personal sovereignty and frees us up from archaic institutions.

Giving governments the ability to print and control money was a huge mistake and now we have to correct it. Absolute power corrupts absolutely. Some examples are Zimbabwe, Venezuela, and the Soviet Union. Money should be independent of the state as proposed by Austrian economic theory.

Bitcoin Offers the possibility of breaking up the coalition between politicians and bankers spreading power to the people in a truly distributed way.

If you think the government (of any color) is going to help you, I have bad news for you, they just can't. It is the system that's broken and unless you get out and write your own destiny, you'll be stuck in useless fights.

Bitcoin makes you free, independent, and responsible. It makes you an adult, unlike the nanny state that treats you like a child. Only those countries that share the power with their citizens are successful. Totalitarian regimes end up badly. Bitcoin helps by removing power from governments and giving it back to their citizens.

Chapter 16

Risk

Investing is always risky. Whether it is real estate, stocks, gold, or cash there is always the possibility of losing money.

Experts talk about the alpha and the beta. Alpha is the potential for gains, while beta is the risk incurred. Usually, the higher the alpha, the higher the beta, and the opposite is also true.

The trick here is to find investments with a decent alpha but with a low beta.

In the case of Bitcoin, most experts agree that it has unlimited upside but limited downside. This makes it the biggest asymmetric bet in our lifetimes.

If you buy $1000 worth of bitcoin, it could go 20x, or 100x but the downside is limited to your initial investment. If you can win $100,000 only risking $1000, that's already an interesting proposition.

The lottery also has a big alpha and a small beta. The problem is that the probability of winning is near zero. With bitcoin, the chances of winning are much higher and the chances of going to zero are less than 1%.

By looking at BTC's history, its growing demand, safety record, and shrinking supply, it is easy to understand why this is only the beginning and why the potential for growth is exponential.

Bonds, for example, are at the other extreme, they have a very small alpha and beta, which is why they can hardly be called an investment.

But something unpredictable could always happen, making the whole thing collapse. This is what Nassim Taleb calls a black swan - unknown unknowns - that could strike at any time, changing everything we think we know. Although black swan events are very rare, it's worth keeping this in mind and avoiding placing all the eggs in the same basket.

Nevertheless, the bitcoin risk has been exaggerated by the media. It has some volatility in the short term but in the long run, the trend is always upwards.

Opportunity cost

Every choice in life comes with an opportunity cost, nothing is free. Keeping your money in the bank makes you lose money that you could have potentially made by investing.

Bitcoin is clearly a better option than real estate, gold, or stocks. This is even more evident when compared to cash.

It's far riskier to hold cash right now than to invest it. Inflation keeps growing and by the time governments come to terms with it, it'll be too late. Whatever you do, get rid of your cash now. It's far too risky.

Dangers

Being a digital asset that lives in the cloud, the dangers for bitcoin come from the security protocols we are able to put in place. By using a cold wallet and following some basic guidelines, these risks can be minimized.

The Internet is a dangerous place for everyone and this includes identity theft, bank account hacking, phishing, and many other perils. This is why keeping your keys offline is paramount.

With Bitcoin, the weakest link is you, so make sure you follow the proper protocols.

Altcoins

Altcoins usually go up faster than BTC but also drop faster during a bear market. With these tokens, the risks are higher.

I don't recommend buying any token below the top 20 but if you do, expect anything.

A safer strategy would be to invest a small percentage of your portfolio in Altcoins and sell them before the end of the bull market in order to buy more BTC and ETH.

Cash

A friend of mine doesn't invest in anything because he deems it too risky. He doesn't realize the opportunity cost of holding cash in an inflationary scenario.

Make sure you educate yourself and invest in the biggest alpha with the lowest beta you can find. Failure to do so will cost you a fortune.

Chapter 17

Bitcoin is your pension

As you've probably guessed by now, the pension system is broken. There is only so much denial we can take. At the end of the day, we must come to terms with reality and accept that our pension will be peanuts.

Whether you are hoping to get a social security payment, a private pension scheme, or a combination of both, you better start looking for Plan B before it's too late.

This is a recent article published by Foxnews:

Social Security funds could run out of money sooner than expected, forecast warns

Medicare will run out of its current funding by 2026, matching previous estimates

Experts have been warning about this for ages. The social security system was poorly designed for an era with very different demographics and now the numbers don't add up.

Private pensions are not any better. They promised defined benefits to sell us the product, knowing that their projections were far off the mark.

It's all a big scam.

If you are near retirement age, it's going to be hard. You might have to find some extra sources of income, side hustles, or monetize a hobby of yours until you build up a nest egg. In any case, start acting now and do an honest review of your financial situation.

But if you have 10 years or longer before retirement then you are still on time to invest. Needless to say that I recommend bitcoin.

I've been worrying about my pension for the last 20 years. Both the public and the private ones are rubbish so I have been looking at alternative investments like real estate and the stock market.

I've done ok..ish but it's not enough. These still won't cover my expenses. Luckily, I found bitcoin, and I no longer worry about my financial future.

With bitcoin, I'm much more confident that my investment will pay off. While the pension is a black hole sucking up financial energy, bitcoin is a treasure chest found on a desert island.

For the last 12 years, it has gone up 6,000,000% and although this rate is probably not sustainable, it is expected that it can easily go 20x from here. Do you think your pension will appreciate 20x? Fat chance.

Everyone is realizing this opportunity and more people and institutions are joining in. Ironically, some of the biggest investors coming to the crypto universe are... yes you got it! pension funds!

They are so ashamed of producing such dismal results that they have decided to diversify into BTC to see if at least they can grow slightly faster than inflation. But don't bother with those. Buy your bitcoin directly and get rid of the middlemen. Those fat cats don't deserve your money.

Like Raoul Paul, a macro investor that owns bitcoin and ETH, I'm irresponsibly bullish on crypto.

Chapter 18

Forecast

Making predictions is a dangerous business, especially in the volatile world of crypto. However, once you study the market, see the potential and the risks, you have to put your money where your mouth is. After all, this is what investing is all about.

With crypto, the trend points clearly upwards, at least with the strong coins, but the timing is extremely hard. I know that bitcoin will get to $1 Million. I just don't know when exactly.

In any case, this game has to be played for the long run. Don't try to time the market or the market will time you out.

If you buy and hodl for 10 years, not only you will make money but you could easily make life-changing wealth.

Predicting the future is somehow compulsory for most professions - doctors, lawyers, engineers - but for some reason economists seem to be the ones less capable of getting it right. So far, most economists have predicted the demise of bitcoin and so far, they have been spectacularly wrong.

The problem with classical economics is that they rely exclusively on Keynesian dogma and bitcoin is more attuned to Austrian economics. For them, it's like reading Chinese, they just don't get it.

Money that is not produced and controlled by the government is anathema to them so that's probably the reason why they remain poor. Ever seen a wealthy economist? Me neither.

Thank God, I'm not an economist so I can make predictions and I'm pretty sure I will get most of them right. Here's my take:

- At the end of this bull market (mid-2022) BTC will get to at least $100,000
- ETH will go to $10,000 in the same period
- In 2030, BTC = $1 Million, ETH = $100,000
- Real inflation will reach 20% annually for the next 10 years
- Bitcoin will become legal tender in most African and Latin American countries
- CBDCs will arrive in 2025 in China, Europe, and the USA. They will be somehow successful but there will be a much stronger parallel economy run on bitcoin
- The blockchain will be ubiquitous with many apps and uses - electronic voting, notary services, digital ID, traceability, CO2 footprint, etc
- Developing economies adopting bitcoin will become developed nations
- Countries rejecting bitcoin will suffer an economic downturn
- Dogecoin and most shitcoins will disappear
- Decentralization will be the most important concept in the 21st century with Dapps, DAOs, and Smart Contracts
- AI will destroy jobs but crypto will create employment and opportunities
- Big nations with oversized power structures will break into smaller decentralized nations
- Bitcoin will become the reserve currency worldwide
- There will be large migrations of people looking for places with a higher quality of life and lower cost of living

- 100% of energy will be green and Bitcoin will be one of the main spurs
- Most banks will either shut down or change dramatically thanks to bitcoin
- Global warming will start recovering and the world will become a much cleaner place
- There will be fewer wars once the petrodollar is out

Predictions were made in October 2021. Let's see how it goes.

Chapter 19

Conclusion

In the 90s, most people didn't know what the internet was. 10 years later it had completely taken over the world. That's the power of technology.

It's hard to notice a revolution when you are in the midst of it but the process follows its course with or without you.

20 years ago, you probably missed the internet revolution but now you have another chance. Don't let another 20 years go by just to realize you've missed out again.

In this time and age, we should have learned from the past and gotten to recognize the signs of disruptive technology. But we haven't. People still think the future will be a small variation of the present, just a little bit faster, just a little bit better.

Bitcoin is a disruptive technology. It will affect banking, wall street, rail payments, and global finance.

The Internet changed the world and bitcoin is disrupting the money world. Everything is affected by money so the changes will be even more profound.

With bitcoin, just by pressing a button, you have access to a whole new world of possibilities. You can invest, borrow, lend and transact. You can use all the services you use now and more only faster, cheaper, and more secure.

With Crypto you can get up to 12% interest on deposits, you can borrow at 1%, you can trade, buy or sell NFTs, use smart contracts or use decentralized applications. Banks are getting worried and quite rightly so.

Even the Fiat money you carry in your pocket now will become obsolete in a few years. The transformation is going to be profound and there is nothing you can do to stop it.

Google, Apple, and Amazon turned the music, book, video, and retail industry upside down by digitizing products and services. Now bitcoin will disrupt the banking industry by digitizing money.

Fiat money, gold, and even real estate do not belong to you. Banks and governments can seize it at any moment with some legal excuse. The only asset that it's truly yours is bitcoin - the only form of unconfiscable money.

Bitcoin is not just a speculative asset to become rich, it's a lot more than that. It's financial independence, it's freedom, it's decentralization. It's a bank for the unbanked, it's hope for the excluded. It's optimism for creating a just world. It's security, transparency, and immutability. It's permissionless and censorship-resistant. It's green energy and the best store of value ever.

Bitcoin is risky like any investment, but fiat money is much riskier, get rid of it asap.

If you are still hoping that the government comes to the rescue this time, I've got bad news for you. Nothing is going to save you this time, you are on your own. The system is broken beyond repair.

They will rescue the banks and those closer to the money printer but not you. Bitcoin is your last chance.

We are about to enter one of the worst economic crises in financial history. COVID-19 has decimated many industries, unemployment is on the rise and the only solution they have is to print more fake money.

You could lose everything you've worked so hard for - your house, your job, your money, and your pension. Don't ignore the perils, don't hide your head in the sand. Wake up and realize what's going on before it's too late.

All your life you have trusted banks, the government, and institutions. Unfortunately, this will not save you this time. The entire system is collapsing. We are witnessing a new world order, technology is affecting everything, China is trying to take over but that's not a world you want to live in.

The only hope is to make the world more decentralized, to redistribute power widely, and to get rid of old oligarchies. We humans are not trustworthy so we better set some limits for those at the top.

This is the reason why Nakamoto created bitcoin, to make the world fairer, more decentralized, and more egalitarian. A system based on Math is more reliable.

You can participate in this new ecosystem in many ways. You could invest, transact, make donations, help people in Africa, code, study, and promote it. Speak to your friends about it. Set up your own node. Embrace freedom.

We are extremely lucky to be witnessing this transformation. This is going to be amazing for everyone but before the calm comes to the storm, we'll have to endure the chaos. A change like this comes with a lot of ripples. Make sure you find a safe haven for yourself and your family. Help others to do the same. Be a leader.

I've written this book to warn you about the dangers and inform you about the opportunities. This is exciting and scary at the same time. Crisis means opportunity in Greek and this is exactly what this is. To make the most of it, you must be on guard, ready, and take action. Don't let the tsunami destroy you.

Living in denial won't help you this time, it's time to face the music and dance.

Be a rebel, not a sheep.

If you have any requests, questions, or critiques please let me know through any of my channels. I promise to answer.

I wish you all the best in your bitcoin adventure and please, share it on social media so that we can all benefit from your perspective.

But remember,

The best time to plant a tree was 20 years ago, the second-best time is now.

Disclaimer:

Nothing in this book is financial advice, do your own research and make your own decisions. Never invest what you can't afford to lose, and always invest for the long run.

All the best.

Printed in Poland
by Amazon Fulfillment
Poland Sp. z o.o., Wrocław